C. S. LEWIS:

Apostle to the Skeptics

C. S. LEWIS: Apostle to the Skeptics

By CHAD WALSH

WIPF & STOCK · Eugene, Oregon

Wipf and Stock Publishers
199 W 8th Ave, Suite 3
Eugene, OR 97401

C.S. Lewis: Apostle to the Skeptics
By Walsh, Chad

ISBN 13: 978-1-55635-883-8
Publication date 11/03/2008
Previously published by The Macmillan Company, 1949

Series Foreword

C. S. Lewis (1898–1963) taught Medieval and Renaissance Language and Literature at Oxford and Cambridge Universities for almost four decades.

He wrote much for publication: literary criticism, poetry, theology, spirituality, science fiction, juvenile literature, novels, autobiography, but alas no plays. Over and above that, he kept up a fierce correspondence for decades; 3,228 letters of his compiled and edited by Walter Hooper have been published in three volumes (2000–2006).

Hooper, long the literary adviser to the Estate of C. S. Lewis, has done much of the primal research on Lewis, editing and seeing to publication perhaps a dozen collections of Lewis's shorter writings (essays, articles, addresses; literary criticism; diaries).

Most Lewis books are still in print in one way or another. But various studies of and commentaries on Lewisiana by others have not had the same longevity. Many are now out of print, but there is much research and review yet to be done.

To aid present and future scholars, Wipf and Stock Publishers has established a series devoted to worthy books on or about Lewis. Perhaps because I have done four books on or about Lewis, Wipf and Stock has asked me to be the general editor of the series.

William Griffin
Series Editor for C. S. Lewis Studies
2007

Acknowledgments

IN THE September 1946 issue of *The Atlantic Monthly* I published an essay entitled "C. S. Lewis, Apostle to the Skeptics." Practically all of it has been incorporated at one place or another in this book. I am indebted to the *Atlantic* for permission to do this.

Chapter 21 ("One Straw in the Wind") is based largely on my article, "A Variety of Writers—and How They Rediscovered God," *The New York Times Book Review,* 18 July 1948. I appreciate the kindness of the editors of the *Review* in allowing me to make use of the essay.

In quoting from the works of C. S. Lewis I have utilized the American editions whenever possible. Most of them were published by the Macmillan Company of New York. I should like to take this opportunity to make a general acknowledgment of my gratitude to them for permitting me to make extensive use of their copyrighted material.

In the case of Lewis's books published by firms other than Macmillan I make individual acknowledgment in the footnotes.

For

Viola C. White

who lent me *Perelandra*

Foreword

"C. S. Lewis, the Oxford don, the pious paradox-monger and audacious word-juggler, will surely meet his match one of these days and be subjected to a severe debunking operation," wrote Victor S. Yarros recently in *The American Freeman.*[1] "He is asking for it. Oh, for a Huxley, or a Heine, or an Ingersoll, to expose his tricks and call his bluffs!"

"At the ingenuity of this book I stand aghast," stated T. V. Smith in his review of Dr. Lewis's recent book, *Miracles.*[2] "But I am not touched by its covert appeal to piety, nor moved to credence by its overt argument. It is modernistic apologetics for Christian fundamentalism."

Meanwhile, critics of a more sympathetic cast have showered the author of *The Screwtape Letters* with superlatives. His mind has been likened to St. Paul's; one enthusiastic reviewer proposed that he be appointed William Temple's successor as archbishop of Canterbury.

When the authorities disagree, and disagree with such heat, one suspects that the subject of their disagreement is worth further study. That is why I have written this book. No Christian apologist in the English-speaking world is today as much talked about and argued about as C. S. Lewis. *The Great Divorce* was recently dramatized over the BBC. Twentieth Century Fox is considering the possibilities of extracting a movie from Screwtape. Dr. Lewis's influence

[1] December, 1947.

[2] *The Saturday Review of Literature,* January 31, 1948.

continues to spread wherever English is spoken, and in the last few years it has spilled over into other linguistic areas. *The Screwtape Letters* have been translated into at least eight languages, including Afrikaans; Polish and Arabic translations are in preparation. Others of his books have gone into half a dozen languages.

That a writer of Dr. Lewis's scholarly and literary stature should publish more than a dozen books directly or indirectly defending Christianity is news; that his works should have such wide repercussions is still more significant news and merits a second thought. What does it mean when his books become best-sellers? Does the fact indicate anything about the intellectual currents of the present decade? If so, its seems time to examine more closely the exact kind of Christianity and philosophy presented in Dr. Lewis's writings, and the literary techniques that have brought him to the forefront of authors dealing with religious themes.

In this book I hope to add something (though not too much) to the scanty supply of biographical information available about Dr. Lewis, but my main concern will be with his ideas, the way he presents them, and the significance of his popularity.

I have many debts to acknowledge. First of all, I am deeply grateful to Dr. Lewis himself for giving me generous stretches of his time when I went to England in the summer of 1948. Via transatlantic airmail he had urged me to desist and devote my time to better subjects (such as some safely dead writer), but once he became convinced that I considered the study worth doing he wholeheartedly coöperated with me. He answered innumerable questions without evasion, and his friendliness did much to make my stay in England enjoyable. I should emphasize, however, that this book is not an "authorized commentary." Most of the information I requested of Dr. Lewis had to do with the brute facts of his life, not the exact interpretation of his writings. If I pass along any misinterpretations to the reader the fault is mine, not Dr. Lewis's.

During my stay in England I visited the offices of a number of Dr. Lewis's British publishers (Geoffrey Bles, John Lane, J. M. Dent & Sons, the Oxford University Press) and in each case was given free access to their files of critical articles and reviews. The notes I was thus enabled to take without painfully searching for needles in a haystack were very valuable, and I deeply appreciate the uniform courtesy and helpfulness extended me.

To Beloit College I am indebted for both moral and financial backing in connection with the trip to England. I should also like to thank Miss Louise Smith and Miss Elaine Smogard, of the Beloit College Libraries, for their enthusiastic assistance and almost magical efficiency in securing from a variety of sources a large number of out-of-print books which I needed for background information.

Finally, I ought to confess that this study would very likely not have been undertaken at all if it had not been for my wife, Eva. Several years ago I published in *The Atlantic Monthly* an essay of the same title as this book, but it was she who passed along to me what she modestly termed her "brain storm": the idea that the essay was worth expanding into a full-length treatment of C. S. Lewis.

CHAD WALSH

Beloit College
November 1948

Contents

1. Briefly Biographical

To students of heredity C. S. Lewis would be an intriguing research problem. His veins flow with a complex blend of aristocratic and peasant blood. The blue blood ("a tiny drop," he insists) is a legacy from his mother's mother, whose descent can be traced to the first Norman invaders, intermingled with old Irish strains. If inclined to such speculations, one might attribute to this heredity the grace of Lewis's style and almost unfailing courtesy with which he presents his opinions, whether by the printed word, over the BBC, or in private conversations.

Lewis's mother, *née* Flora Augusta Hamilton, was the daughter of a naval chaplain and possessed many clerical relatives. This fact constitutes the one similarity to the other side of the family. Lewis's paternal great-grandfather (son of a Welsh small farmer) was an amateur preacher in his youth. The grandfather, Richard Lewis, was of a wandering nature; he drifted first to Cork as a master boilermaker, then to Dublin, and eventually to Belfast, where he settled and became the co-proprietor of a small shipyard.

The student of heredity might at this point observe that the Welsh strain (coupled with clerical inclinations on both sides of his family) accounts for Lewis's evangelical zeal and the courage he displayed during World War II when he did what few chaplains would dare attempt—

delivered lectures on elementary theology at RAF bases in England. Such theories are tantalizing, but forever unprovable, and I gladly abandon them for the prosaic facts of biography.

To return to Lewis's paternal ancestors—his father, Albert James Lewis, continued the slow climb of the family by becoming a solicitor at Belfast. From his marriage with Flora Augusta Hamilton two children resulted: W. H. Lewis (later to reach the rank of major in the regular Army, and now retired), and a second son, Clive Staples Lewis, born in November of 1898.

His mother died when Lewis was about nine (his father lived until 1929). Even as a small boy, Lewis was of a pessimistic cast of mind. The early death of his mother deepened the pessimism and threw him back on the resources of literature and his own imagination. In a letter to his publishers he says of that period:

> I was a younger son, and we lost my mother when I was a child. That meant very long days alone when my father was at work and my brother at boarding school. Alone in a big house full of books. I suppose that fixed a literary bent. I drew a lot, but soon began to write more. My first stories were mostly about mice (influence of Beatrix Potter), but mice usually in armor killing gigantic cats (influence of fairy stories). That is, I wrote the books I should have liked to read if only I could have got them. That's always been my reason for writing. People won't write the books I want, so I have to do it for myself: no rot about 'self-expression.'

In another letter he comments on his Celtic blood, adding the disappointing statement, "the Celtic origin seems never to have affected my imagination which is Germanic through and through—Norse mythology having been my first love and perhaps my strongest."

Such is the picture we piece together of Lewis as a boy: lonely, imaginative, reading the books that filled a big empty house, writing tales of his own, dwelling on the myths of the Eddas, viewing the work-a-day world with the black pessimism that was later to be one of the weightiest reasons for his renunciation of Christianity.

He left home to be educated at a succession of boys' schools, most of which he cordially detested, though he gratefully remembers one excellent classics master at Malvern College. Meanwhile, he crossed the frontier from doubt to definite atheism. He was fourteen at the time. When I asked him to analyze the reasons why he tossed over the Anglican Church in which he had been reared—and with it Christianity in general—he recalled three main factors. In the first place, at one school which he attended the matron was a dabbler in spiritualism and theosophy. Lewis became excited at her ideas, which had the charm of novelty. He did not actually embrace her faith, but it attracted him sufficiently to engender a vague feeling that there is no definite body of dogma which one must believe—that in any event the truth does not lie in the familiar doctrines of Christian orthodoxy. Perhaps still more important, the problem of pain—later to supply the title and subject for one of his books—already tormented him. He was sensitively aware of the heartlessness of man to man and the cruelty of the natural world. He could not reconcile what he saw with belief in a good and omnipotent God. The world seemed a "bad show," and God either foolish or wicked.

The third reason for Lewis's "conversion" to atheism reveals the interests of the future scholar. On reading the Latin and Greek classics he discovered that the men of antiquity believed in many gods, but all the editors of text-books took it for granted that these gods never existed. He found the same thing when he studied the Norse gods and later turned to Celtic mythology. With plausible logic he reasoned that if the pagan gods were merely myths it was highly probable that the Christian God was also a myth.

After leaving Malvern College he became a private pupil of an Ulsterman, W. T. Kirkpatrick, the former headmaster of Lurgan College in Ireland. Lewis's father had studied there as a boy. Young Lewis, now an excited atheist, was delighted to discover in Kirkpatrick a kindred soul. Any-one curious to know more of Kirkpatrick will find him, suitably altered for artistic reasons, in the person of the dour but lovable Scotch skeptic, MacPhee, of *That Hideous Strength.*

The lasting thing that Lewis gained from the association was ruthless training in honest habits of thought. "A rigid logician," he describes Kirkpatrick. By one of those ironies which seem more the rule in life than the exception, the fiercely logical methods of reasoning that Lewis learned from the Ulsterman were many years later to be the principal road leading back to Christianity.

In late 1916 Lewis received a scholarship to University College, Oxford. He came for the summer term in 1917, but was there only a short while before he volunteered for the Army, and entered it as a second lieutenant. He reached the front lines on his nineteenth birthday, and was plunged into the fighting around Arras and Lillers. His career as a soldier was abruptly ended by an English shell that fell short, inspiring the famous remark of his aunt, "Oh, so *that's* why you were wounded in the back!"

After hospitalization he spent considerable time in various convalescent camps. He was demobilized in December 1918. In January of the next year he was back in Oxford, where he began the "greats" course (classics). He received a First in "honor moderations" (the midway examinations), and another First in "greats," the final examinations. Next he "did the English schools," receiving still another First and his A. B. in 1923. Several years later he was awarded his master's degree, which at Oxford comes from continued residence and study but does not require the formality of additional examinations.

Such was his university education. It followed the well-worn path of any Oxford student interested in classics, except that his work in the English schools gave him a grounding (later to be very useful) in English literature and philology.

To anyone knowing Lewis when he returned from the war he must have seemed merely a gifted student with a bit more imagination than the average. It is true that in 1919 he published a volume of verse, *Spirits in Bondage*, but it was quietly lost in the great sea of "new poetry" then at flood tide. The prospects of earning a living as a poet seemed dubious when he received his A. B., and, like many another poet, he was glad to get a position teaching. His opportunity came in 1924 when E. F. Carritt secured a year's leave of absence to lecture on philosophy at the University of Michigan. Lewis was employed to substitute for him.

A permanent position opened up at the end of the year of philosophy, but in another field. In 1925 Lewis became a fellow and tutor in English language and literature at Magdalen College, where he has been ever since. A year later he published a long narrative poem, *Dymer,* which attracted more attention than the first volume but did not make his work familiar to the compilers of popular anthologies.

The next few years contain little of public interest. Like any other Oxford don he was kept busy tutoring his dozen or so pupils and preparing lectures. But it was a time that was to yield an exciting harvest in the next decade. His further reading in medieval and Renaissance literature laid the groundwork for several outstanding books in literary history and criticism. More important for our purposes here, it was during the 1920's that he was, very reluctantly, inching his way back toward the Christianity that he had repudiated at the age of fourteen.

To trace the process step by step is not possible. I doubt whether Lewis himself could do it, for such a change in outlook is seldom reached as neatly as a problem in geometry is solved. But the main stages are clear.

It was primarily the doing of his restless mind, sharpened to the demands of logic by the good atheist, Kirkpatrick. In the Preface to the 1943 edition of *The Pilgrim's Regress* Lewis says that his intellectual progress was from "popular realism" (*i.e.,* if you kick a brick you know it's real) to philosophical idealism, then to pantheism, then to theism, and finally—with much hesitation—to Christianity. ("I'm not the religious type," he once wrote when asked for personal data. "I want to be let alone, to feel I'm my own master: but since the facts seemed to be the opposite I had to give in.") The clearest record of this philosophic pilgrimage is contained in the *Regress*—though presented in a somewhat generalized and depersonalized fashion. Echoes of it are found in many of his books. For example, the sections confuting pantheism in *The Case for Christianity*[1] and *Miracles* reflect the ideas troubling Lewis some years earlier when he stood on the threshold of theism.

His mind drove him to Christianity, but the heart also had its role. I shall have to discuss this in more detail later, when I deal with Lewis's peculiar use of the word "Romanticism"; for the moment it is enough to note that his quest was not unlike that of the German romanticists pursuing the Blue Flower. He plucked one blossom after another and saw it turn to a weed in his hands; finally he learned from his own experience that only in Christianity could he reach the strange, elusive object of his quest.

There were, of course, the influences—personal and literary—along the way. Only a few years after his solemn acceptance of atheism he fell quite accidentally under the spell of George Macdonald, whose books have ever since been the most influential in Lewis's religious and literary development. As Lewis describes the momentous encounter:[2]

> It must be more than thirty years ago that I bought—almost unwillingly, for I had looked at the volume on that bookstall and rejected it on a dozen previous occasions—the Everyman edition of *Phantastes*. A few hours later I knew that I had crossed a great frontier. I had already been waist deep in Romanticism; and likely enough, at any moment, to flounder into its darker and more evil forms, slither-

[1] Published in England as *Broadcast Talks*.

[2] From *George Macdonald: An Anthology*, pp. 20–21. Copyright, 1947, by The Macmillan Company and used with their permission. Published in England by Geoffrey Bles, Ltd.

> ing down the steep descent that leads from the love of strangeness to that of eccentricity and thence to that of perversity. Now *Phantastes* was romantic enough in all conscience; but there was a difference. Nothing was at that time further from my thoughts than Christianity and I therefore had no notion what this difference really was. . . . What it actually did to me was to convert, even to baptize . . . my imagination. It did nothing to my intellect nor (at that time) to my conscience. Their turn came far later and with the help of many other books and men.

Another literary influence of considerable importance was G. K. Chesterton, whom Lewis eagerly read despite his obvious Christianity. Among personal friends, several anthroposophists (followers of Dr. Steiner) indirectly prepared him for theism by their critique of materialism.

Whatever the exact details of the long-drawn-out process, the official capitulation can be dated. In 1929, at the age of thirty, Lewis became a theist and shortly thereafter once more a communicant of the Church of England.

For a man to throw over his religion in childhood and return to it in adult years does not make the headlines. Though perhaps not as common an experience as college chaplains wistfully contend, it is frequent enough. And Lewis resisted any temptation to rush his spiritual adventures into print. It was not until four years later, in 1933, that he published the *Regress*, which, because of the obscurity of its references and the complexities of allegory, was not widely read at the time.

Meanwhile the other Lewis—to make an artificial distinction—burst on the scholarly scene with *The Allegory of Love*—a study of the medieval tradition of courtly love and the evolution of the allegorical form which so satisfyingly filled a gap in scholarly literature that it was almost universally acclaimed by the specialists and was awarded the Hawthornden Prize in 1936.

He published a couple of other scholarly books in the next few years, and several works dealing directly or indirectly with theology, but his real leap into public attention dates from 1941 when *The Screwtape Letters* began to appear serially in *The Guardian.* The BBC rushed him to the microphone and for two or three years his was one of the most familiar voices in England. Each of his twenty-nine radio broadcasts was heard by an audience estimated at 600,000. The same talks, later published as three slender books, have reached a further huge public.

During World War II he also gave his famous lectures on theology at RAF bases, followed by question-and-answer periods. The assignment was little to his taste ("I certainly never intended being a hot gospeler," he said. "If I had only known this when I became a Christian!") but he stuck doggedly to it. Meanwhile his books, ranging from fantastic novels to formal theological treatises, poured from the English and American presses, two or three sometimes being published in a single year.

Lewis's popular reputation as a theologian received scholarly recognition in 1946 when he was awarded an honorary degree of Doctor of Divinity by St. Andrews University, in Scotland.

Now that the war is over and he no longer feels duty-bound to ride the circuits of RAF bases his daily life has returned to more of its old pattern. The post-war influx of students has greatly stepped up his tutorial duties; he has notified the BBC that he is not available for further broadcasts during the foreseeable future.

At present he is writing his memoirs, but does not venture a guess as to when they will be completed. When I talked with him in Oxford he had reached the end of World War I. He is also doing the volume on English literature of the sixteenth century (exclusive of the dramatists) for the projected Oxford History of English Literature. (His literary interests, he says, have gradually shifted from the Middle Ages to a slightly later period.) He talks vaguely of completing a children's book which he has begun "in the tradition of E. Nesbit." The Student Christian Movement Press, in its recent announcement of forthcoming books, listed a text on semantics, *Language and Human Nature,* to be written jointly by Lewis and his friend, Prof. F. R. R. Tolkien, but I gather that it is still in the blueprint stage.

Patently Lewis has not written himself out, but the books he has in mind suggest that he is taking a holiday from the kind of writing that has created his public reputation. His admirers busily urge various theological topics upon him, but so far as I know he has no immediate plans for further works of apologetics.

Such are the bare bones of biography. And there I might leave it, since I am inclined to share Lewis's own belief that one should study a writer's books rather than his personality. But Lewis's books in themselves convey so remarkably clear an impression of Lewis the man that I cannot forbear supplementing them by one further chapter before turning from the man to his books.

2. The Man

When I took the boat train from Plymouth and started on the first lap of my journey to Oxford I found myself musing on the contrast between Lewis's books and the picture of him which frequently adorns the dust-jackets of the same books. The books had wit and grace. The picture was sad-eyed, world-weary. I could not fit picture and books together.

None of the thumb-nail sketches vouchsafed me by friends who knew Lewis had solved the mystery. One said he looked like a Welsh farmer; another compared his appearance to that of a benign Anglican bishop; a third stated that both in features and manner he was the *avatar* of Dr. Johnson.

Only after I met Lewis did I see that the solution to the enigma was simpler than the theories I had been busy devising. He consented to pose for a couple of snapshots and I perceived that—like half of humanity—he stands stiffly at attention and freezes into impersonality when a camera is pointed his way. The picture on the dust-jackets resembles him about as much as a mummy resembles a living man.

I understand, too, why my friends found it exceedingly difficult to characterize Lewis. It is not that his physical appearance is hard to put into words. He is medium height, stocky, has a very ruddy face with a network of fine veins just beneath the surface. His eyes are dark, and so is the hair that is now retreating from his forehead and has almost vanished from a large spot on the top of his head. Such are the anatomical details. But to convey the total impression that he leaves with you is much more difficult.

His most striking trait is the aliveness of his face. His expression changes, lights up, as he talks or listens. He has a quick smile which I would call "sweet" if the word did not have too feminine a ring for one of the most masculine persons I have ever known; the smile is curiously akin in spontaneity to W. H. Auden's, though otherwise Lewis bears no resemblance to the lanky, Viking-like poet.

No one seems to have instructed Lewis in the formal art of public relations. I never detected him pausing to phrase a reply carefully for fear it might be used against him. If I mentioned prominent names he commented on them with matter-of-fact candor (whether favorably or no) and did not add that this was "off the record." When I inquired his opinions on a vast variety of matters he answered with equal directness—though sometimes his response was simply, "I don't know enough to have an opinion."

It adds up to plain unselfconsciousness. One reason, I believe, is that he still has no real conception of how widely his books are read and how familiarly his name is bandied about. No doubt his publishers send him itemized statements of his sales, and I am equally sure that he tosses them into the waste-basket. (He keeps no scrapbook of reviews, I discovered to my regret.) To the world outside of Oxford he is a famous figure. To himself he is an Oxford don who writes an occasional book in odd moments.

The comparison with Dr. Johnson has a grain of truth in it, as I discovered to my cost. Lewis—at least on the occasions when I was with him—never crushed an opponent with the brusqueness of Boswell's hero, but he has a sharp, quick-moving mind, impatient of vagueness and half-formed ideas. He is swift to press home his advantage when somebody begins talking without fully thinking out what he is talking about. Such was my experience when I tried to defend surrealist art. Next day I thought of many excellent arguments, but at the moment I could offer nothing except thoughts in the process of gestation, and Lewis expertly pushed me to the wall and left me pinned there. However, the manoeuvre is performed so smoothly, and in such a friendly, manly way, that it seems a compliment and act of respect. And Lewis, when occasionally pushed to the wall himself, can admire the skill of the pusher.

When Lewis talks, he often reminds you of his books, particularly the broadcast talks. He is straight to the point, never at a loss for the exact word. A sly, ironic humor flashes through, though not steadily. His books are more witty than his conversation. Ordinarily he expresses himself with urbanity, but occasionally he forsakes the rapier for the battle-axe. I remember one time he narrated a conversation he had had with some psychology-minded friends. They had spent the entire evening discussing sex in the language of the clinic—"release for tensions," etc. Suddenly Lewis burst out, "If a visitor from Mars had overheard them he would never have suspected that sex has any connection with pleasure! They made you think of skeletons copulating. Sometimes you want to teach such people vice so that they can know what virtue means."

His memory is a highly selective one. You can hardly quote any fragment from the classics or medieval and Elizabethan literature without seeing his face light up with recognition, but he refers you to *Who's Who* if you ask for the date of his graduation from college or a complete list of his books.

He dresses as one would expect: not with bohemian eccentricity, not with Beau Brummel fastidiousness, but with a casualness that approaches but never quite reaches the point of carelessness. His most distinctive article of dress is a tan-colored fisherman's hat, which he frequently loses. I recall seeing him pause in front of a bush in one of the parks of Magdalen College and suddenly exclaim, "This looks like my hat." He plucked the hat from the bush, tried it on, and walked on murmuring, "This must be my hat."

Lewis is not a "joiner." So far as I know, his name does not appear on the letterhead of any organization designed to reshape England or the world. He is sociable, but in a personal way. He prefers to drink beer and chat with a small group of close friends rather than revel in the artificial fellowship of the large get-togethers that modern gregarious society so generously provides.

"I like monotony," he once told a reporter, and I suspect that his daily routine varies little. In "term-time" he sleeps in college, arises in time to tackle his voluminous correspondence from 9:00 to 10:00 (he seldom leaves a fan-letter unanswered, no matter how asinine its contents), takes his pupils, one or two at a time, from 10:00 to 1:00 and again from 5:00 to 7:00. His writing and preparation of lectures are crammed into the early afternoon hours and the evenings.

During the vacations he varies his customary routine by sleeping at home—a rambling, twelve-room brick house at Headington, a suburb of Oxford—and usually may be seen working in the morning in the Bodleian from 9:30 to 1:00. With no pupils to tutor he finds himself freer to enjoy the company of his friends and work on whatever book he happens to be writing at the moment.

Anyone who has marveled at Lewis's profuse output can find a partial explanation in the fact that he is blessed with great facility. He ordinarily writes out a manuscript in longhand, makes a few changes between the lines, and then turns it over to a professional typist to be made ready for the publisher.

His college rooms are in what is sometimes called the "new building." (It merely dates back to the eighteenth century.) To reach them you ascend Stairway 3 and enter Room 3—a large, handsome, white-paneled reception room, where he usually confers with his pupils. In cold weather, when fuel runs short, the conferences are shifted to the small inner study, a book-crammed room with a fireplace. From the windows he has a good view of the tame deer of Magdalen Park meekly enduring the curiosity of tourists.

The stretch of time from 11:00 to 1:00 on Tuesday mornings Lewis ordinarily manages to keep free so that he can join a small circle of close friends at a certain small, sedate pub, which I have promised to leave nameless so that the ravenous public will not storm it for the delectable cider that is its speciality. There, in a private parlor, he and the half a dozen others pass an hour or two conversing on everything from the nature of God to the latest University events. This particular group dates back to the war years when the Oxford University Press (whose headquarters are normally in London!) fled from the blitz to Oxford, and one of its staff, Charles Williams, became the center of a little circle which met Tuesday mornings at the pub and Thursday evenings in Lewis's college rooms.

Charles Williams died in 1945, but the Tuesday morning meetings continue. The group is a fluctuating one. It is likely to contain a couple of Lewis's colleagues such as Professor Tolkien, one or two students, sometimes a relative of someone or a distant friend. Once, as I remember, a small farmer from Shropshire was present and wittily entertained the company with a tirade against A. E. Housman. "Lads don't commit suicide any more frequently in Shropshire than in other counties," he insisted, and Lewis, from the storehouse of his selective memory, recited the famous parody: [1]

What, still alive at twenty-two,
A clean upstanding chap like you?
Sure, if your throat is hard to slit,
Slit your girl's and swing for it.

Like enough, you won't be glad,
When they come to hang you, lad.
But bacon's not the only thing
That's cured by hanging from a string.

When the blotting-pad of night
Sucks the latest drop of light,
Lads whose job is still to do
Shall whet their knives and think of you.

Only in retrospect did I realize how much intellectual ground was covered in these seemingly casual meetings.

[1] I have been unable to discover who the author is. Mr. Lewis suggests that Housman himself may have written it.

At the time the constant bustle of Lewis racing his friends to refill empty mugs or pausing to light another cigarette (occasionally a pipe) camouflaged the steady flow of ideas. The flow, I might add, is not a one-way traffic. Lewis is as good a listener as talker, and has alert curiosity about almost anything conceivable—including such linguistic minutiae as the American distinction between "homely" and "homey."

Women have not figured prominently in this description of Lewis's social life. The fact that he is unmarried and that he once stated in an autobiographical sketch, "There's no sound I like better than adult male laughter," suggests a certain preference for the society of men. The myth-makers, ever eager to provide human-interest material, have invented further details. A particularly persistent legend, which has found its way into *Current Biography,* has it that Lewis is so shy in the presence of women that he frequently locks himself in his room when they appear at the college. I had occasion to call the story to Lewis's attention several years ago when I was writing an article about him, and he replied: "The pleasant story about my locking myself in my room when a woman invades the college precincts is—I regret to say—pure bosh. For one thing women are wandering through 'the college precincts' the whole blessed day. For another, having taken female pupils of all ages, shapes, sizes, and complexions for about twenty years, I am a bit tougher than the story makes out. If I ever have fled from a female visitor it was not because she was a woman but because she was a *bore,* or because she was the fifteenth visitor on a busy day."

I cannot imagine Lewis quailing at the sight of a skirted figure (and his novels show considerable understanding of female psychology), but it is true that Oxford, despite the presence of women students, is still a man's world and has a lingering flavor of the monkish past hovering over it. Lewis, like most of his colleagues, finds the greater part of his social and intellectual life with men.

I have said that Lewis is not a "joiner." There is, however, one organization in which he is very active. That is the Socratic Club. Started by Miss Stella Aldwinckle half a dozen years ago, it meets every Monday evening in term, and has from sixty to a hundred members—chiefly undergraduates—plus a number of hangers-on who come to the occasional open meetings. The original purpose was to have a paper read defending some aspect of Christianity one week, and an atheistic paper the next, but, as Lewis states it, "We discovered there was an undersupply of atheists willing to speak without pay." Thus in practice too many of the papers (Lewis believes) have been pro-Christian or have dealt with comparative religion.

The papers are followed by a discussion period, in which Oxford students and fellows—traditionally adept at unsparing criticism—do their best to tear down the arguments they have just heard. Chapters from several of Lewis's latest books were originally read before the Club, and he utilized the gruelling of his intellectual adversaries to tighten up his own reasoning and anticipate the objections likely to arise in the minds of readers.

In the days of Charles Williams occasional small meetings on vacation mornings served a similar purpose. Lewis read *Perelandra* chapter by chapter to the assembled group, and Williams read his final novel, *All Hallows' Eve.*

To form an accurate opinion of how Lewis is regarded in Oxford is not easy. For one thing, he lives as inconspicuously as possible, and Oxford is inclined to coöperate with anyone's desire to avoid the limelight. The barmaid at one of his favorite pubs spoke of him with great respect, but to her he was simply "Mr. Lewis at Magdalen College." She was astounded to learn that he had written books.

The bookstores of Oxford, when I was there, had none of his books displayed in the windows. I made discreet inquiries of the clerks, and was told by some of them that his works sold so fast they were often out of stock, while others implied that his theological writings had created a sensation a few years ago but Oxford had now recovered from the shock.

Among the book-store clerks, and still more among professional scholars, I encountered some sad shaking of the head because Lewis has not devoted himself exclusively to literary research. One of the editors of the Oxford University Press praised *The Allegory of Love* in the most unrestrained language and added that Lewis's subsequent career had been one long decline and fall. Beyond doubt, many other scholars wish the gifted shoemaker had stuck to his last.

The clergy and thoughtful laymen, on the other hand, live in fear that he will revert to writing scholarly books on literature. As they see it, a halt in his output of popular apologetics would be a disaster to Christianity in England. Among clergymen I found almost universal enthusiasm for his work, though sometimes tempered, if I am not mistaken, by an all too human trace of envy and jealousy. One priest accused him of oversimplification—of seeing everything "black and white"—and deplored the fact that on two separate occasions Lewis had preached in Congregational churches in Oxford "at the very hour when High Mass was being celebrated in Anglican churches." (Lewis has preached a number of times in Oxford's numerous Anglican churches, and always to huge congregations.)

General rumor has it that Lewis is considered a formidable enemy by the "progressive element" of the Oxford faculty—particularly those who are infected with what Robert Hutchins calls "scientism." He is especially distasteful to the logical positivists, who have been much in evidence at Oxford since the mid-1930's and whose cold, science-based system of thought is the direct antithesis of the warm humanism of Oxford. That Lewis reciprocates the distaste is clear from his description of Wither, one of the demonically possessed characters in *That Hideous Strength:* [2]"He had passed from Hegel into Hume, thence through Pragmatism, and then through Logical Positivism, and out at last into the complete void."

Everywhere I heard that Lewis's lectures are the best attended of any at Oxford. His deep, easy, powerful voice, the lucidity of his presentation, the intermittent wit—coupled with the intangible thing called personality—packs the hall when he appears. Many times he has been obliged to announce that all who are "reading English" will be seated first, then other students, and then (if any room is left), the general public.

Meanwhile, Lewis goes his relaxed and active way. A close friend to a few, a famous name to many, he moves among the familiar scenes of Oxford with the ease of long habit and the sureness of a man who knows what he is doing: whether walking to the pub, the lecture hall, or church.

[2] P. 420. Copyright, 1946 by Clive Staples Lewis. Used by permission of The Macmillan Company, publisher. Published in England by John Lane.

3. Over the BBC

> *Everyone has warned me not to tell you what I'm going to tell you in these talks. They all say 'the ordinary listener doesn't want Theology; you give him plain practical religion.' I have rejected their advice. I don't think the ordinary listener is such a fool.* —*Beyond Personality*, p. 1.*

Lewis's books fall into half a dozen different types. The easiest reading—though not the most entertaining—is offered by three volumes scarcely thicker than pamphlets. Their pages appeal to the eye by a friendly profusion of contractions; the sentences are short and pointed; the language has a minimum of theological and technical terms.

These three books—*The Case for Christianity, Christian Behaviour*, and *Beyond Personality*—owe their chattiness to the fact that they are slightly altered transcripts of several series of broadcasts which Lewis delivered over the BBC. In the Preface to the first volume he explained: "I gave these talks, not because I am anyone in particular, but because I was asked to do so. I think they asked me chiefly for two reasons: firstly, because I am a layman, not a clergyman; and secondly, because I had been a non-Christian for many years." He might have added that an excellent speaking voice (a deep baritone) and the ability

* From *Beyond Personality*. Copyright 1945 by The Macmillan Company and used with their permission. Published in England by Geoffrey Bles, Ltd.

to handle abstract reasoning in down-to-earth language contributed to the sensational success of the series.

The Case for Christianity does not attempt to follow Aquinas' multiple-approach proof of the existence of God. Lewis concentrates exclusively on the "moral argument." To demonstrate that a sense of Right and Wrong is universal he shows human nature in action. "Everyone has heard people quarrelling," he writes, and then quotes the typical outcries: "That's my seat, I was there first"—"Leave him alone, he isn't doing you any harm"—"Give me a bit of your orange, I gave you a bit of mine"—"How'd you like it if anyone did the same to you?"

Each squabbler is appealing to some standard of conduct and seems to assume that his adversary knows about the same standard—and is violating it. Back of the Moral Law there must be a Lawgiver—such is the assumption that Lewis develops in several tightly knit broadcasts. A chain of reasoning of this sort encounters greater skepticism than would have been the case two hundred years ago, when the idea of an innate moral sense still prevailed even among thinkers who had rejected Christianity. The anthropologists, with their records of strange customs and incomprehensible tabus, have spread a vague feeling that morality differs so much from place to place that it is impossible to speak of "Moral Law" in the abstract.

Anticipating this objection, Lewis argues [1] that different cultures "have only had *slightly* different moralities. Just think what a *quite* different morality would mean. Think of a country where people were *admired* for running away

[1] From *The Case for Christianity*, p. 5. Used by permission of The Macmillan Company. Published in England by Geoffrey Bles, Ltd. under the title, *Broadcast Talks*.

in battle, or where a man felt *proud* for double-crossing all the people who had been kindest to him. . . . Men have differed as to whether you should have one wife or four. But they have always agreed that you mustn't simply have any woman you liked."

A second argument often brought against universal Moral Law is that what we call morality is merely herd instinct. Lewis readily admits that the instinct exists, but contends that there are other instincts in conflict with it. If you see a man drowning, your herd instinct tells you to rescue him, but the instinct of self-preservation says to stay safely on the shore. The deciding vote is not cast by any one instinct but by something that sits above the warring instincts and passes judgment on them: in other words, by awareness of the Moral Law.

Having explained why he believes in the Moral Law, which is implanted in each individual, Lewis points out that it differs completely from the natural laws of science. The "law of gravitation" means that if you drop a stone, it has to fall. The Moral Law, on the other hand, is not what men always do but what they ought to do. This leads to the disconcerting realization that we are obligated to obey a Law we did not create, that we violate it constantly, and that we are at war with the Lawgiver. On that grim note the first half of the book ends.

The second half is an admirably concise summary of orthodox Christianity, with strong emphasis on the doctrines that modern thought finds least palatable: the divinity of Christ, Original Sin, Heaven, Hell.

The book was naturally hailed with delight by the orthodox, while the Modernists admired Lewis's literary skill but not his theology. The Reverend John Haynes Holmes, of the community church in New York, cried out in protest:[2]

> After an excellent analysis of atheism, pantheism, and theism, he passes on to an almost incredibly naive statement of Christian theology. "An evil power (Satan) has made himself for the present time the Prince of this World." . . . Jesus Christ, who if not God in the flesh is either a lunatic or an imposter, has borne the punishment of man's sin, and thus made possible his deliverance from the Evil One. In due course God (Christ) will come again, invade and conquer the world, and destroy Satan and those who still side with him.

The next book in the broadcast series, *Christian Behaviour*, plunges without further ado into a statement of the Christian attitude toward ethics.[3] "Morality . . . seems to be concerned with three things. Firstly, with fair play and harmony between individuals. Secondly, with what might be called tidying up or harmonising the things inside each individual. Thirdly, with the general purpose of human life as a whole: what man was made for. . . ." By this definition he breaks with the popular concept of morality, which restricts the word to type one (the "social" and "anti-social" school of thought) or is willing at most to add a few postscripts on "individual adjustment" and "integration."

Lewis elaborates his theme with a directness almost unique in modern books on Christian ethics. The average Christian apologist, endeavoring to win the dubious world

[2] *The New York Herald Tribune,* November 14, 1943.

[3] From *Christian Behaviour,* p. 2. Copyright, 1943 by The Macmillan Company and used with their permission. Published in England by Geoffrey Bles, Ltd.

over to an exacting system of morality, has in recent years resorted to hedging, "reinterpretation," loopholes, and a loving emphasis on the "spirit of morality" at the expense of the letter. The neutral terminology of psychology has also frequently been pressed into service to avoid the forbidding connotations of the Christian moral vocabulary. Lewis makes none of these gestures of appeasement. He boldly employs words like *chastity* and *sin,* and tells the emancipated citizens of the twentieth century: [4] "There is no getting away from it: the old Christian rule is, 'Either marriage, with complete faithfulness to your partner, or else total abstinence.' " In the chapter on marriage he comes out bluntly for the rule of no divorce as far as Christians are concerned, and—with even greater daring—says that wives should obey their husbands.

If Lewis leaves no loopholes in the Christian doctrine of sex and marriage, he does succeed in making the obligation to love your neighbor as yourself seem a trifle less impossible than it appears at first glance. He distinguishes sharply between *loving* and *liking.* You can love your neighbor (that is, wish him well just as you wish yourself well) without feeling the faintest trace of liking for him, and without trying to pretend that he has no faults. Love, in the Christian sense, is an act of the will, not of the emotions, and the Christian is not obliged to manufacture feelings to accompany it.

Almost all Christian reviewers received the book well, though there were occasional complaints that the picture of morality was too static and leaned too much on past codifications. A vehement reaction from the other side of

[4] P. 25.

the fence was provided by Alistair Cooke, writing in *The New Republic:* [5]

> In the days before radio, Mr. Lewis' little volume would have been reviewed politely in the well bred magazines and no harm would have been done. But the chief danger of these homilies on behavior is their assumption of modesty. They are talks given over the radio by an Oxford don fairly recently converted to Christianity. From the way they were received in Britain, and from the eagerness of American networks to have Mr. Lewis shed the light on our own dark continent, it may be assumed that the personal values of several million Britons and Americans stand in imminent danger of the befuddlement at which Mr. Lewis is so transparently adroit. Mr. Lewis has a real radio talent. . . .
>
> . . . The exposition of every fundamental human problem from "Social morality" to "Marriage" and "Charity," comes out with a patness that murders the issues it pretends to clarify.

The most theological of the three volumes, and at the same time the one most devotional in tone, is *Beyond Personality.* Its peculiar intensity and unyielding dogma led *Punch* to ask,[6] "Is theology really so hellish?" *The Times Literary Supplement* noted the buoyant enthusiasm of the book: [7] "Mr. Lewis has a quite unique power of making theology an attractive, exciting and (one might almost say) an uproariously fascinating quest." *The Friend,*[8] while ad-

[5] April 24, 1944.
[6] "Accuse Not Nature . . .," October 11, 1944.
[7] "Theology as Discovery," October 21, 1944.
[8] Review by C. F. Carter, November 17, 1944.

mitting that "Friends will be grateful . . . for many challenging remarks in this book," was troubled by its theology: ". . . I cannot believe that C. S. Lewis's theology was Christ's theology. It does not bear the essential simplicity of eternal truth."

The book turns out to be primarily about two things: the Trinity and the difference between "nice people" and "new men."

The Trinity has always been a stumbling block to Christian apologists. The problem is to explain how three divine "Persons" can exist without being three Gods. Lewis, avoiding the technical definitions of the Council of Chalcedon and the Athanasian Creed, resorts to analogies: [9] "In God's dimension, so to speak, you find a being who is three Persons while remaining one Being, just as a cube is six squares while remaining one cube. Of course we can't fully conceive a Being like that: just as, if we were so made that we perceived only two dimensions in space we could never properly imagine a cube."

All three Persons of the Trinity are pictured in action as an ordinary Christian kneels down to say his prayers: "He is trying to get into touch with God. But if he is a Christian he knows that what is prompting him to pray is also God: God, so to speak, inside him. But he also knows that all his real knowledge of God comes through Christ, the Man who was God—that Christ is standing beside him, helping him to pray, praying for him."

The last half of the book is devoted to showing that Christianity does not aim merely at developing "nice people": the goal is "new men"—new, because a different and higher kind of life (which Lewis calls *Zoe* to distinguish it

[9] P. 10.

from biological life, *Bios*) has been brought into being in them by their utter surrender to Christ.

In none of Lewis's books are the difficulties of being a Christian driven home more ruthlessly, and in none does he succeed in making the goal more alluring. With shrewd insight into the modern mind he turns to evolution in order to explain what Christianity is all about. The "new men" are presented as the next stage in evolution—or rather, as the stage that part of humanity has already reached: [10]

> . . . the Christian view is precisely that the Next Step has already appeared. And it is really new. It isn't a change from brainy men to brainier men: it is a change that goes off in a totally different direction—a change from being creatures of God to being sons of God. The first instance appeared in Palestine two thousand years ago.

The final pages of the book emphasize once more the price: [11] "But there must be a real giving up of the self. You must throw it away 'blindly' so to speak. Christ will *in fact* give you a real personality: but you mustn't go to Him for the sake of that." And in conclusion one hears the voice of George Macdonald speaking through the Oxford don: [12] "Keep *nothing* back. Nothing that you have not given away will ever be really yours. Nothing in you that has not died will ever be raised from the dead. Look for yourself, and you will find in the long run only hatred, loneliness, despair, rage, ruin, and decay. But look for Christ and you will find Him, and with Him everything else thrown in."

This seems a convenient place to mention Lewis's most

[10] P. 62.
[11] P. 67.
[12] P. 68.

recent book, which though not based on radio broadcasts, is a transcript of the spoken word. *The Weight of Glory and Other Addresses* [13] consists of three sermons preached in Oxford and two speeches before secular groups. The volume has no particular unity, and is chiefly of interest as revealing several of the strands of thought that figure prominently in Lewis's more massive works. (It is also calculated to make the average minister or priest envious of anyone privileged to preach in erudite Oxford, where it can be assumed that the congregation has an excellent cultural background. Lewis is here considerably more "intellectual" than in his broadcast talks.)

The first of the five addresses and the most moving piece in the collection is "The Weight of Glory," a sermon on Heaven and the inborn hunger for Heaven. It usefully supplements several treatments of the same subject in Lewis's other books.

The second of the five addresses is "Transposition"—nominally a discussion of the religious phenomenon of "speaking with tongues," but really concerned mostly with the theory that when a higher form of experience is expressed through a lower medium a certain ambiguity always results. Thus Pepys, upon hearing exquisite music, felt sick at his stomach. The concept of "transposition" is interestingly if sketchily applied to the Incarnation and the resurrection of the body.

"Membership" is the one place, so far as I know, where Lewis dwells in some detail on the Christian concept of the Mystical Body of Christ and contrasts it both with modern

[13] This book is to be published by The Macmillan Company in the fall of 1949. Published in England by Geoffrey Bles under the title *Transposition and Other Addresses*.

individualism and modern collectivism. It also contains his rationale for democracy and the legal fiction of equality: they are justified not because men are good but because they are all part of a fallen race and it is dangerous to entrust great power to any one individual.

"Learning in War-Time" develops two ideas. One is that the crisis of war is not so great as the perennial crisis faced by us all as we walk the knife-thin ridge between Heaven and Hell. The second contention is that Christianity does not eliminate the ordinary activities of human life; instead, it throws them into a new perspective. The Christian is not to give up "culture"; he is to work humbly at it (if such is his vocation), "as to the Lord."

The final address, "The Inner Ring," is a word of advice to undergraduates at King's College, London, warning them of the perils and frustrations of trying to break into one charmed circle after another. It is most meaningful if read in conjunction with his novel, *That Hideous Strength.* The moral of the address is that the attempt to be an insider is self-defeating; the only kind of recognition that has abiding significance is that based on honest workmanship.

4. Into Deeper Waters

> *What we learn from experience depends on the kind of philosophy we bring to experience. It is therefore useless to appeal to experience before we have settled, as well as we can, the philosophical question.*
> —*Miracles*, p. 11.*

Lewis was an immediate success as a radio popularizer, but the medium must have imposed a painful discipline upon him. In three of his other expository books—composed not for the microphone but the printing press—he could assume a more leisurely frame of mind, and willingness to grapple with ideas that cannot be adequately presented in measured particles of radio time. *The Problem of Pain, Miracles,* and *The Abolition of Man* contain a greater amount of original thought than the radio talks and are meant to be digested more slowly.

The Problem of Pain has proved a favorite with the theologians. It deals with one of the tormenting facts of the universe that drove Lewis into childhood atheism. In the introductory chapter he analyzes the three basic ingredients of all advanced religions: (1) The sense of "numinous awe" in the presence of the supernatural, illustrated by Ovid's picture of the dark grove on the Aventine or the words of Jacob, rising from sleep, "How dreadful is this place." (2)

* From *Miracles*. Copyright, 1947 by The Macmillan Company and used with their permission. Published in England by Geoffrey Bles, Ltd.

Morality—and the awareness of frequently disobeying it. (3) "The third stage in religious development arises when . . . the Numinous Power to which they feel awe is made the guardian of the morality to which they feel obligation." [1]

The fourth strand in religion is unique to Christianity: an historical event. This, of course, is the appearance of Jesus, who claims to be in some way identical with the Numinous Power which is the sanction of Morality. Here, according to Lewis, the real problem of pain arises. Christianity teaches that God loves mankind so greatly that He died an agonizing death for mankind's sake—this is the assurance that the Numinous Power is *good*. Yet, pain exists everywhere in the world and often without any apparent purpose. How to reconcile a good God and pain?

Lewis's attempt to solve the intellectual difficulties leans heavily upon the doctrine of Original Sin. Man, as created by God, was in perfect harmony with his Creator until the fatal promptings of pride (perhaps implanted by the Devil) led him to disobedience. As Lewis imagines it, the Fall very likely involved biological consequences in addition: the direct command that the earliest men may have had over the organs of the body was lost; disease, senility, and death entered the picture.

Since the Fall the supreme problem of every human being has been to reëstablish the relationship with God that originally existed: complete and joyous obedience. To do this means a kind of death to our warped impulses. As long as things go smoothly we prefer to drift along without facing the alternatives. Pain and tribulation are God's megaphones: they wake us up to reality.

Lewis does not pretend that this line of reasoning, which

[1] From *The Problem of Pain*, p. 10. Used by permission of The Macmillan Company. Published in England by Geoffrey Bles, Ltd.

I have summarized too quickly for full justice, explains everything. There is still the question why two people very similar in other ways are afflicted with different degrees of pain and tribulation. So far as I can see, no Christian writer—or writer of any other persuasion—has ever made the whole picture of pain intellectually and morally tolerable. Lewis's theory covers a great deal of ground, but perhaps needs to be supplemented by what seems at first sight a wild suggestion—though I believe Lewis himself at one point hints at its possible value. I am thinking of the idea advanced by Dr. E. W. Adams [2] that *some* at least of the pain in the world is not the voice of God but the sport of the Devil. This explanation, of course, only pushes the mystery back one step, but it does have the merit of tallying with what seems the incurably pluralistic nature of reality.

The chapters on Heaven, Hell, and Animal Pain we shall have to consider at more length later on. That on Animal Pain is of particular interest as betraying the limitations of viewpoint encouraged by the pleasant civilization of orderly Oxford, but for the moment we must turn to a book more ambitious in its scope and clear-cut in its aims—*Miracles: A Preliminary Study.*

If the existence of seemingly unmerited and fruitless pain is an emotional obstacle to the acceptance of Christianity, the plentiful miracles of the New Testament are an intellectual stumbling block. The modern mind has been shaped by the picture of a mechanical universe operating according to uniform and unvarying laws.

By an ironic coincidence, Lewis's book on miracles appeared at about the same time as Dr. Barnes's *The Rise of Christianity,* affording the reviewers the delightful specta-

[2] "The Problem of Pain as a Doctor Sees It," *The Hibbert Journal,* January 1944.

cle of an Anglican bishop busily explaining away the miraculous while an Anglican layman labored to put firm philosophic props under it.

In no other religion is the question of miracles so crucial as in Christianity. The Buddhist may admit that the birth narratives associated with Gautama are late fables and be in no way troubled by the admission: Gautama never claimed to be more than a human teacher. But orthodox Christianity rests upon one supreme miracle—the Incarnation—and the Gospels are interlarded with lesser invasions by the supernatural. It is very difficult to take the scissors and cut out the miracles without removing everything else at the same time. As Canon Eric Montizambert has soberly expressed it:[8] "The matter of extreme significance is that usually in St. Mark, and very often elsewhere, *the great messages of Jesus are by Him deliberately built upon an immediately preceding miracle in an integration so complete that separation is impossible without destruction of the lesson's point*" [italics his].

Miracles is "a preliminary study"—an attempt to decide on philosophic grounds whether miracles are theoretically possible. It does not include any effort to pass judgment on the individual miracles recorded in the Bible, nor to master the complex textual problems involved.

Lewis divides mankind into two groups: the naturalists and the supernaturalists. The first believe that the material universe is all there is. It is a vast, self-existent process, every detail interlocking with every other detail. The whirling of the atoms and the poet's raptures are merely parts of the total show, subject to the same over-all causa-

[8] *Christianity in Crisis*, The Cloister Press, Louisville, Kentucky, 1945, pp. 111–112. By permission of the publishers.

tion. The supernaturalist, on the other hand, is convinced that something or somebody exists outside the visible universe and is able to intervene.

Using as his weapon the *reductio ad absurdum,* Lewis attacks naturalism. If everything is the blind result of the total process, then one thought is as good as another, and there is no reason for believing that one *-ism* (such as naturalism) is more valid than another.

Having established that the existence of thought (or at least belief in its value) demands belief in something outside the closed system of the physical universe, Lewis takes up the question of what other kinds of supernatural intervention (miracles proper) may be expected. Assume that this something (*i.e.,* God) is capable of miracles, would He ever choose to exercise his power, and if so, when?

Lewis's criterion is the application of a sort of esthetic-religious sense. Miracles, he says,[4] "are not exceptions (however rarely they occur) nor irrelevancies. They are precisely those chapters in this great story on which the plot turns. Death and Resurrection are what the story is about; and had we but eyes to see it, this has been hinted on every page, met us, in some disguise, at every turn, and even been muttered in conversations between such minor characters (if they are minor characters) as the vegetables."

The concluding chapters are written with the greatest feeling and poetic power. I know of no better modern treatment of the Incarnation than "The Grand Miracle." "Miracles of the Old Creation" and "Miracles of the New Creation" are highly successful attempts to show the "propriety" of the New Testament miracles.

[4] P. 119.

"The people who may well be assisted in the extension of their credulity are those who have already swallowed the Divine Camel but shrink from a miraculous gnat," wryly commented W. J. H. Sprott in *The New Statesman.*[5] In general the book has trod on more toes than did *The Problem of Pain* and provoked more spirited reactions. Friendly critics praised the purpose of the work but deplored some of its details. Fundamentalists and Roman Catholics [6] found themselves in agreement that Lewis had fallen into heresy by his statement that some of the Old Testament miracles might be viewed as an expression of truth "in mythical form," in contrast with Truth becoming historically incarnate in the person of Christ. But in general, as one would expect, the orthodox joyfully hailed the book, and the Modernists and agnostics sharpened their pens for it.

The Abolition of Man does not properly belong with the two preceding books, nor with any others that Lewis has written. I am including it here because it is important and is no more out of place here than anywhere else. His purpose this time is not to prove the existence or attributes of God but simply to establish that the *Tao* (or Natural Law or Traditional Morality) is absolute and unchangeable, and that if it is overthrown the upshot will be the destruction of man as man and his assimilation by "Nature."

The book—as slender as *The Case for Christianity*—is based on the Riddell Memorial Lectures, which Lewis delivered at the University of Durham in 1943. The impres-

[5] May 31, 1947.

[6] See, for example, *Books on Trial,* December–January 1947–48.

sive subtitle expresses the ostensible purpose: "Reflections on Education with Special Reference to the Teaching of English in the Upper Forms of Schools." Lewis's whipping-boys are two text-books written for use in English elementary schools. The books are of a sort perhaps even more familiar to American school teachers than to British: they seize on the popularized findings of semantics to debunk all "value judgments."

The two texts, though subjected to a merciless analysis at Lewis's hands, are merely the convenient springboard from which he launches his attack on all attempts to explain away morality. His argument is simply that morality (which is much the same in all civilizations) is like the axioms of geometry—unprovable because basic and obvious. To the contention that a new morality should be evolved, based (say) on one's obligation to society, he answers that[7] "From propositions about fact alone no *practical* conclusion can ever be drawn. *This will preserve society* cannot lead to *do this* except by the mediation of *society ought to be preserved.*" With the word "ought" the old *Tao* reënters by the side door.

Another suggestion—that instinct should be the basis of morality—is countered with the question, "Which instinct?" It can be seen that the book is in large measure an amplification of the ideas treated in the first part of *The Case for Christianity,* but here the purpose is not to vindicate God but to vindicate morality itself. The title suggests the future of mankind if all concepts of objective morality

[7] From *The Abolition of Man,* p. 20. Copyright, 1947 by The Macmillan Company and used with their permission. Published in England by Geoffrey Bles, Ltd.

are destroyed. Humanity would first turn into a race of "men without chests"—that is, without any store of emotions organized by habit into dependable sentiments. The liaison between the "brain" and the "belly" would be destroyed.

"Nature" would then proceed to regain all the ground she has lost to man. With no categorical imperatives to guide him, with no real belief in the efficacy of thought, man would respond to the casual urges of weather, digestion, any irrational factor. Lewis believes that the process is already far advanced. In a paragraph foreshadowing the main theme of his three novels he points out the linguistic signs: [8]

> The process which, if not checked, will abolish Man goes on apace among Communists and Democrats no less than among Fascists. The methods may (at first) differ in brutality. But many a mild-eyed scientist in pince-nez, many a popular dramatist, many an amateur philosopher in our midst, means in the long run just the same as the present rulers of Germany. . . . The belief that we can invent 'ideologies' at pleasure, and the consequent treatment of mankind as mere ὕλη, specimens, preparations, begins to affect our very language. Once we killed bad men; now we liquidate unsocial elements. Virtue has become *integration* and diligence *dynamism*, and boys likely to be worthy of a commission are potential officer material.' Most wonderful of all, the virtues of thrift and temperance, and even of ordinary intelligence, are sales-resistance.

[8] P. 46.

5. The Myth-Maker

> *Most myths were made in prehistoric times, and, I suppose, not consciously made by individuals at all. But every now and then there occurs in the modern world a genius—a Kafka or a Novalis—who can make such a story.*
>
> —Preface to *George Macdonald: An Anthology*, p. 16.

C. S. Lewis is a good expository writer but a better myth-maker. In his myths he has complete freedom to be not only a theologian and philosopher but also a prose poet and creator of a new universe.

Out of the Silent Planet, *Perelandra*, and *That Hideous Strength* were issued as "novels," but in reality they are three instalments of one myth. In form, they resemble the interplanetary fiction of H. G. Wells and the "scientifiction" of American pulp magazines, but there is a clear difference. Lewis's novels are the scientifiction of a philosopher.

The shortest and most Wellsian of the books is *Out of the Silent Planet*. The hero, Ransom—a Cambridge philologist who bears a suspicious resemblance to Lewis—is kidnaped by Devine (a gold prospector) and Weston (a half-mad physicist who wants to extend humanity and its misery to the utmost bounds of the universe). The captors load Ransom into their spaceship and take him to Mars, meaning to turn him over to the "natives" as a human sacrifice in order to win their good will and coöperation.

It turns out that the two adventurers have completely misjudged the Martians. When Ransom escapes from his companions and comes to know the inhabitants of the planet at first hand he finds that their way of life is so peaceful that the adjective "bent" is their nearest equivalent for "evil." There are three species of *hnau* (rational beings), all living together in great harmony. The most appealing of the Martian races is the *hrossa* (plural of *hross*). Six or seven feet in height, they are [1] "something like a penguin, something like an otter, something like a seal." They fish, practice a primitive agriculture, and spend their leisure hours reciting poetry in choral formation.

The brain trust of the *hnau* consists of the *séroni* (plural of *sorn*)—tall, lean creatures like elongated men, their legs covered with feathers. They are without passion or poetry; their days are devoted to scientific research and the supervision of the simple technology of the planet.

The *pfifltriggi* (plural of *pfifltrigg*) are froglike beings, who work as miners and artisans. They can construct any device at demand, provided only that the blueprints prepared by the *séroni* are complicated enough to make the task interesting.

The *hnau* are not the only inhabitants of Malacandra—the "Old Solar" name for Mars. Spiritual beings called *eldila* (plural of *eldil*) move about and take a benevolent interest in the life of the Martians. The natives recognize their presence readily enough; to Ransom they appear only

[1] From *Out of the Silent Planet*, p. 55. Used by permission of The Macmillan Company. Published in England by John Lane.

as a faint movement of light. The ruler of the planet is Oyarsa, a super-*eldil*, who handles the rare instances of insanity or criminality by magically "unbodying" the disturber of the peace.

Oyarsa is merely the deputy of the invisible Maleldil, who is none other than the Second Person of the Trinity, and worshipped as such by all the Martians. Indeed, one of the first acts of the *hrossa* is to instruct the pious Ransom in the elements of true religion.

Interspersed with Ransom's wanderings are descriptions of the strange, lovely landscapes of the old planet. Life is now confined largely to the valleys warmed by the water of artificial canals; the high plateaus, which millions of years ago supported a teeming population, are frozen and airless. In a few more million years all life will come to an end, a prospect that the Martians, obedient always to Maleldil's will, discuss philosophically.

Malacandra has what can only be called a planned society. There has been no catastrophe similar to the disobedience of Adam and Eve—the ever-watchful Oyarsa, with his unbodying rod, is alert to preserve the divine harmony between Maleldil and *hnau*. The world is an archaic one, created by Maleldil before He had determined to make the daring experiment of granting complete free will to any of His creatures.

Ransom, greatly marveling that such love and coöperation prevails among the varied *hnau* of Malacandra, learns that this is the normal way of life in the solar system. The earth is the exception. Because of the rebellion of Adam and Eve (prompted by the Oyarsa of the earth, who for some mysterious reason went bad), the earth has been cut off from direct communication with the uncorrupted planets, and it is called Thulcandra—"the silent planet"—in token that its Oyarsa takes no part in interplanetary conferences.

There is little plot to the book. Ransom, after many wanderings and philosophic conversations, finally reaches Oyarsa's court. Shortly thereafter he sees Weston and Devine being led in captive. (They had wantonly murdered a *hross.*) Weston, asked to defend himself, indulges in pompous rhetoric. Ransom's attempt to translate his speech into Old Solar (which was the language of the earth, also, before the Tower of Babel episode) results in some passages of delightful irony, such as: [2]

> 'I may fall,' said Weston. 'But while I live I will not, with such a key in my hand, consent to close the gates of the future on my race. What lies in that future, beyond our present ken, passes imagination to conceive: it is enough for me that there is a Beyond.'
>
> 'He is saying,' Ransom translated, 'that he will not stop trying to do all this unless you kill him. And he says that though he doesn't know what will happen to the creatures sprung from us, he wants it to happen very much.'

Oyarsa decides that Weston and Devine don't know any better. He orders them back to the earth; to Ransom he gives the opportunity to stay on Malacandra, but Ransom casts his lot with his companions and joins them in their hazardous but successful space-ship voyage back to poor old Thulcandra.

Though *Out of the Silent Planet* is the slightest of the three novels, it has a naïve appeal, rather like a Walt Disney animated cartoon with philosophic overtones. Of the two

[2] P. 149.

remaining books, *Perelandra* is perhaps the most perfect and certainly the most hauntingly beautiful. It is the story of "Paradise retained." Ransom is summoned by the *eldila* to an unknown destination, and transported thither in a sort of celestial coffin. Upon arrival he finds himself on Perelandra (Venus), a delicious world of floating islands, glowing colors, friendly heraldic beasts, and exquisite fruits. He feels that he is in Paradise, and discovers that he actually is. God has just created the human race on Venus —one man and one woman, similar in appearance to earthly *hnau* except that they are bright green in color. The Adam of Venus is away on an exploring expedition, but Ransom soon encounters the Eve in all her naked green innocence.

Ransom, contrary to the reader's immediate expectation, feels only reverence and solicitude toward the lovely green lady sharing the floating islands with him. It is not long before he discovers why he has been summoned to Perelandra. Weston, traveling alone this time, arrives in his space-ship. The bent *eldil* of Thulcandra has taken possession of the great physicist and is using him as an instrument to bring about the downfall of the new Eve. (Maleldil has evidently told the Oyarsa of Perelandra to stay on the sidelines and let the inhabitants of the planet exercise complete free will.)

For over a hundred pages the two men match words and wits amid the sensuous beauty of the landscape. Weston tries to persuade the green woman to stay overnight on one of the "fixed lands" (a non-floating island)—the one thing that Maleldil, in order to test her obedience, has forbidden. Ransom counters by narrating the dire results of the terrestial Eve's disobedience. The green woman proves much harder to corrupt than the forthright Eve of

Paradise Lost, but as the chapters fly by, Weston begins to gain ground by the subtlety of his arguments. He has almost convinced the woman that Maleldil really wants her to show some spirit by having a mind of her own when Ransom decides that the matter has gone past the power of words to help. He takes to his fists and leaps at Weston, who by now has so hideously diabolic an appearance that the sight of his face almost paralyzes the Cambridge philologist.

The struggle is long and bloody and does not end until Ransom smashes his enemy in a final bout inside an underwater cave. After a long recuperation from the wounds he has suffered, Ransom departs for the earth, the grateful words of the Adam and Eve still ringing in his ears.

The beauty of the book cannot be more than suggested by a swift summary. The landscape of Venus is so sensuously real that it has already broken into verse. A recent poem in *The Atlantic Monthly* [3] referred to "sun of shadow and light/On a lost perelandran lane." Although Lewis, in his Preface, states that none of the human characters is allegorical, it is hard to escape the feeling that Ransom, the redeemed man, is at least a "little Christ" to the green folk of Perelandra.

Just before his departure from the uncorrupted paradise Ransom has a long conversation with the Adam of Venus, and is told that exciting events may be expected on earth in a few years. There are signs that the final struggle is approaching; the earth may be delivered from evil, and contact reëstablished between it and the other planets.

Armageddon, or at least the dress rehearsal for Arma-

[3] Daniel J. Berrigan, S. J., "Failure," May 1948. Quoted by permission of *The Atlantic Monthly.*

geddon, comes in *That Hideous Strength.* Dealing, as it does, with this fallen world its tone is grimmer and drabber than either of the other novels. Structurally it is by far the most complicated. Great chunks of melodrama and mythology are mixed together, to the bewilderment of many readers.

The main plot is simple enough. The bent *eldil* (*i.e.,* the Devil), with his shrewd understanding of popular psychology, has led his earthly allies to organize the N. I. C. E. (National Institute of Co-ordinated Experiments), which then endeavors to gain control of England (in time, the whole world) under the pretext of carrying forward the twin banners of science and progress. If the attempt is successful, hell will be incarnate on earth; man will be "abolished" and replaced by automata obedient to the will of Satan.

Assorted spirits of darkness, called macrobes (not microbes) speak through the guillotined head of a murderer and direct the operations of the N. I. C. E. The forces of light are led by Ransom, now golden-haired and endowed with changeless youth from his stay on Perelandra. He, too, is in touch with supernatural forces, but his allies are the good *eldila* from other planets.

The two central characters are Mark Studdock, a weak, ambitious, confused young fellow in sociology at Bracton College, and his wife, Jane, a pretty bluestocking who some day is going to finish her thesis on John Donne's vindication of the body. Mark is lured to the N. I. C. E. and then alternately flattered and terrorized into remaining. Actually, the powers of Satan want him only as a step toward getting possession of his wife, who is gifted with second sight and who would be an invaluable means of checking up on what is happening in strategic places—for example, the underground tomb of Merlin, where the great magician has lain in a state of suspended animation for almost fifteen hundred years.

Jane, however, joins Ransom's group. Thanks to her visions the good forces are able to make contact with the resuscitated Merlin, who puts his magic arts at their disposal and uses them to bring the vile schemes of the N. I. C. E. to nought. The climax is achieved amid the roaring of wild beasts, the crash of earthquakes, and other apocalyptic events. For the immediate future, at least, England is safe. As for Ransom, he prepares to journey back to Perelandra, which alone can heal the wound he received in his heel when Weston bit him during their death-struggle.

If the three novels are taken together they present a memorable and dramatic picture of the struggle between good and evil, and the impossibility of remaining neutral. But they do more. They create a mythology of the solar system that makes the vast distances of astronomy tolerable to the imagination. Maleldil is as much present on Mars or Venus as the earth; the space between the planets is not "cold, interstellar space" but "Deep Heaven," alive with *eldila* and the presence of God.

Even so devout a Christian poet as T. S. Eliot shivers at the distances of astronomy: [4]

O dark dark dark. They all go into the dark,
The vacant interstellar spaces, the vacant into the vacant,

[4] *Four Quartets*, Harcourt, Brace and Co., New York, 1943, p. 14. By permission of the publishers. Published in England by Faber & Faber.

but Lewis the Myth-Maker will have none of this. His hero, Ransom, muses during his trip to Mars: [5]

> A nightmare, long engendered in the modern mind by the mythology that follows in the wake of science, was falling off him. He had read of 'Space': at the back of his thinking for years had lurked the dismal fancy of the black, cold vacuity, the utter deadness, which was supposed to separate the worlds. He had not known how much it affected him till now—now that the very name 'Space' seemed a blasphemous libel for this empyrean ocean of radiance in which they swam. He could not call it 'dead'; he felt life pouring into him from it every moment. . . . No: Space was the wrong name. Older thinkers had been wiser when they named it simply the heavens. . . .

The critics have treated the three novels all too casually. They cannot be judged as novels: they are a vast myth. Lewis has baptized the solar system and filled it with the radiant presence of Maleldil.

I shall not be so bold as to apply to Lewis the words he used to characterize Macdonald (cited at the head of this chapter), but I venture the prophecy that the interplanetary trilogy will be one of the few myths of the century that will firmly grip the imagination of future writers and provide them with a treasure trove of symbols.

[5] *Out of the Silent Planet,* pp. 29–30.

6. Dreams and Letters

> *"A dream? Then—then—am I not really here, Sir?"*
>
> *"No, Son," said he kindly, taking my hand in his. "It is not so good as that. The bitter drink of death is still before you. Ye are only dreaming. And if ye come to tell of what ye have seen, make it plain that it was but a dream. See ye make it very plain. . . ."*—*The Great Divorce*, p. 131.*

Three of Lewis's books which employ unusual literary genres are *The Pilgrim's Regress, The Screwtape Letters,* and *The Great Divorce.*

The first-named (subtitled: *An Allegorical Apology for Christianity, Reason and Romanticism*) will never supplant *The Pilgrim's Progress.* It lacks the simplicity and eloquent naïveté of Bunyan; it is also disappointingly empty of the wit and grace that readers of the later Lewis have come to expect. The style is heavy and wooden; the allegorical figures heavier and more wooden. And the reviewers, who bestowed a few pats on the head of the young author, complained with some justice that the book was obscure.

The *Regress* is an allegory within the framework of a dream-vision. The narrator (never named and of no importance) has a dream in which he observes the inter-

* From *The Great Divorce.* Copyright, 1946 by The Macmillan Company and used with their permission. Published in England by Geoffrey Bles, Ltd.

minable adventures of the hero, John, in his flight from Puritania (a land of grim but hypocritical religion, which resembles a satirist's caricature of Ulster). John, in several dozen short chapters, pursues the never-never vision of beauty and joy that haunts him. He tries all solutions: women, artistic movements, various schools of philosophy. Finally, with the aid of Reason, he is led to Mother Kirk, who makes him realize that his desire can be fulfilled only in Christianity, which he accepts by leaping into a deep pool and coming up through an underwater tunnel. Now a twice-born man, he retraces his steps, and sees the scenes of his earlier adventures in a radically different light. At the end, firm in the faith, he crosses the Brook (death), to the accompaniment of indifferent verse sung by the angelic Guide.

When Lewis edited the allegory for the 1943 edition [1] he added a Preface pointing out two of the principal defects: [2] "needless obscurity, and an uncharitable temper." The temper had been directed mainly against the "counter-romantics" (such as the Neo-Scholastics and the American "Humanists") who professed to debunk the complex emotional experience which Lewis labels "Romanticism." The book is also an attack on the "subromantics" (such as the followers of Freud and D. H. Lawrence) but they are treated with more charity.

Mediocre as a work of literature, the *Regress* is invaluable for anyone tracing the development of Lewis's ideas. Practically all his later books exist within it in embryonic form. His belief in orthodox Christianity, his conviction that both "Romanticism" and Reason lead the quester to Christianity, many of his attitudes toward literary and

[1] Geoffrey Bles Ltd., London.
[2] P. 5. By permission of the publishers.

philosophic movements—all appear in an early and incomplete form.

A much more successful use of an unconventional technique is *The Screwtape Letters,* which exploded in book form on the English literary scene in 1942 and soon bounded across the Atlantic.

The admirers of Lewis are divided into two groups: those who have read the *Letters,* and those who have read some of his other works in addition. The book has solved the gift problem for countless thousands. I know of a government office in Washington where *The Screwtape Letters* is almost invariably chosen when the girls arrange a birthday party for one of their number.

Ministers have preached from the *Letters,* and sent marked copies to parishioners in need of specific spiritual counsel. The critics, of almost every viewpoint, have loaded it with superlatives. Leonard Bacon [3] called it "this admirable, diverting, and remarkably original work," and added, "there is a spectacular and satisfactory nova in the bleak sky of satire." *The Manchester Guardian* [4] stated: "The book is sparkling yet truly reverent, in fact a perfect joy, and should become a classic."

The Screwtape Letters, then, have been adequately praised. Lewis, I suspect, is sometimes irked at the disproportionate fame of the infernal correspondence. He has confessed that writing it serially for the *Guardian* grew to be a "terrible bore," and when I talked with him he said that it was far from being his favorite.

However, I have no desire to battle the whole weight

[3] "Critique of Pure Diabolism," *The Saturday Review of Literature,* April 17, 1943.

[4] February 24, 1943.

of critical and popular opinion. The *Letters* are very good indeed, in a very specialized way. They afford little scope for their author's poetic or myth-making ability, but they reveal his psychological insight and his satire at their sharpest.

The *Letters* purport to be written by His Infernal Excellency Screwtape to his young demon assistant Wormwood, who is stationed on the earth. Wormwood's mission is to undermine the faith of a recent convert to Christianity—a pallid, feckless young man, rather like a christianized Mark Studdock. Screwtape bestows a great wealth of shrewd advice on the inexperienced tempter. Wormwood, being new at the job, is inclined toward dramatic techniques, but Screwtape, with the wisdom of many victories, advises him: [5]

> It does not matter how small the sins are provided their cumulative effect is to edge the man away from the Light and out into the Nothing. Murder is no better than cards if cards can do the trick. Indeed the safest road to Hell is the gradual one—the gentle slope, soft underfoot, without sudden turnings, without milestones, without signposts. . . .

The book seems calculated to accomplish two things. First of all, Lewis uses the wisdom of Hell to turn the tables on disparagers of Christianity. Screwtape's knowing advice in the very first letter takes for granted that modern thought, such as philosophic materialism, is based not on reason but emotion, and warns Wormwood against any action that would tempt the patient into using his own mind.

[5] From *The Screwtape Letters*, pp. 64–65. Used by permission of The Macmillan Company. Published in England by Geoffrey Bles, Ltd.

The other purpose of the *Letters* is to encourage the wavering Christian by showing him that his uncertainties are nothing unique, and in all likelihood are planted in his mind by agents of Our Father Below.

The epistolary pattern makes it possible for Lewis to take swipes at many of his pet aversions by the simple expedient of having Screwtape praise them. A hasty glance through the *Letters* will reveal that the Historical Method, flippancy (as distinguished from joy, fun, and the joke proper), "pacifism-and-Christianity," the "historical Jesus," and various fashions in feminine beauty are all targets for witty condemnation.

Quite unintentionally, it may be, Lewis accomplished in *The Screwtape Letters* what he conspicuously failed to do in *The Pilgrim's Regress*—he rivaled Bunyan.The temptations of the patient, and his eventual victory over the team of Screwtape and Wormwood, are the twentieth-century equivalent of the salvation of Christian, as told by the good seventeenth-century tinker.

When *The Great Divorce* appeared in 1946 the dust-jacket of the American edition hopefully described it as "brilliant symbolism very like the author's famous 'Screwtape Letters.'" No blurb-writer has ever missed the mark more sadly. The two books are alike only in the acute psychological insight that both reveal.

The Great Divorce was not received with the same unmixed delight that greeted the *Letters.* It is too disturbing for easy enjoyment. The theme might well be George Macdonald's warning: "No. There is no escape. There is no Heaven with a little Hell in it." Or to quote Lewis's own words, from the Preface: [6]

[6] P. v.

> Blake wrote the Marriage of Heaven and Hell. If I have written of their Divorce, this is not because I think myself a fit antagonist for so great a genius, nor even because I feel at all sure that I know what he meant. But in some sense or other the attempt to make that marriage is perennial. The attempt is based on the belief that reality never presents us with an absolutely unavoidable "either-or"; that, granted skill and patience and (above all) time enough, some way of embracing both alternatives can always be found; that mere development or adjustment or refinement will somehow turn evil into good without our being called on for a final and total rejection of anything we should like to retain. This belief I take to be a disastrous error. You cannot take all luggage with you on all journeys; on one journey even your right hand and your right eye may be among the things you have to leave behind.

Throughout the book the drastic "either-or" is being forced upon the reader. There is very little sugaring of humor and satire to kill the bitter taste, and the beauty of the fantasy somehow only deepens the solemn feeling that, as the angel says to one of the characters,[7] "This moment contains all moments."

The plot amounts to little. Like *The Pilgrim's Regress,* the story is a dream-vision, but there the resemblance ends. The dreamer is Lewis himself, who does not discover he is dreaming until near the end of the book.

In the first chapter the narrator is wandering through the endless streets of a drab, gray town, likened by some of the British reviewers to Manchester. He boards a bus and gradually discovers that everyone there—including him-

[7] P. 101.

self—is a transparent ghost. The entire company travel to the borders of Heaven and are given the opportunity to remain permanently. Most of them decline the offer because they cannot bear to make a clean-cut break with their favorite sins. The greater number are afflicted with some form of pride or self-centeredness, which is more precious to them than all the joys of Heaven. An artist who can think only of artistic movements and his reputation decides on the return trip, as does a woman who insists on dominating her son even after death. The only ghost with the courage to surrender his vice and stay in Heaven is a man guilty of lust—a quiet confirmation of the traditional Christian hierarchy of sins, which considers the sins of the flesh as less deadly than pride.

Each of the ghosts is met by one of the "solid people" who reasons with it and tries to prevail upon it to stay. Beyond these largely futile dialogues there is little action. The setting of the story is of great loveliness: the outlying provinces of Heaven resemble the landscapes of Perelandra.

The high point comes when Lewis encounters [8] "a very tall man, almost a giant, with a flowing beard"—George Macdonald—who, Virgil-like, explains some of the mysteries of Heaven and Hell to his disciple and commands him to inform his readers that everything he has seen is part of a dream and not to be taken literally.

One feels that *The Great Divorce* is the work of a man distinctly older than the rollicking author of *The Screwtape Letters.* The greater and more obvious seriousness is reflected in the sharper diversity of critical opinion. *The Providence Sunday Journal* [9] was bored: "Basically, 'The

[8] P. 60.
[9] May 5, 1946.

Great Divorce' is a sermon cast in the form of an allegory. It's a good sermon, but as allegory it's full of straw-men and cloudy symbolism." (Lewis, incidentally, insists with some vehemence that the book is a fantasy, not an allegory: none of the characters stands for anything else.) *The New Yorker*, on the other hand, said that [10] "If wit and wisdom, style and scholarship are requisites to passage through the pearly gates, Mr. Lewis will be among the angels."

John F. Dwyer, writing in *Thought*, commented that [11] "you feel the joy and happiness of the Bright Spirits, you share their keen pity for the foolish, self-willed ghosts who are their own damnation," while A. C. Deane, in *The Spectator*, goes to considerable length to damn Lewis for lack of compassion: [12] "The metallic hardness of its tone, its air of disdain, untouched by sympathy, for the various weaknesses of human nature. . . . The 'Ghosts,' as the excursionists are called, meet 'Spirits' from heaven who argue with them deftly but in vain. The narrator seems, as it were, to place each Ghost in turn on the lecture-table, to exhibit with deliberate skill his special follies and impenitence, and then to drop him back whence he came."

This charge—lack of compassion—has been leveled against some of Lewis's other books. As though anticipating it, he has Macdonald say: [13]

> "Son, son, it must be one way or the other. Either the day must come when joy prevails and all the makers of misery are no longer able to infect it: or else for ever and ever the makers of misery can destroy in others the happi-

[10] March 16, 1946.
[11] December 1946.
[12] "A Nightmare," January 25, 1946.
[13] P. 124.

ness they reject for themselves. I know it has a grand sound to say ye'll accept no salvation which leaves even one creature in the dark outside. But watch that sophistry or ye'll make a Dog in a Manger the tyrant of the universe."

With these words Macdonald brings Lewis—and the reader—back to the pitiless theme of the book: "no Heaven with a little Hell in it." The air-raid siren that wakes Lewis might better be the warning bell that troubled John Donne on his sick-bed: "And therefore never send to know for whom the *bell* tolls; it tolls for *thee*."

7. The Poet

Like many other authors, Lewis began as a poet and has ended as a prose writer. Most of his poetry dates from his interim period, after he had forsaken Christianity and before he returned to it.

His two volumes of verse were published under the pseudonym of Clive Hamilton. The first, *Spirits in Bondage* (1919), passed almost unnoticed; the second, *Dymer* (1926), received more notice from the critics, who commended its theme if not its absolute poetic worth. *Dymer* is a long narrative poem (nine cantos) in Rime Royal, the stanza form used by Chaucer in *Troilus and Criseyde*. It recounts the deeds of a hero of that name who was born in the "Perfect City"—[1]

> There you'd have thought the gods were smothered down
> Forever, and the keys were turned on fate.
> No hour was left unchartered in that town,
> And love was in a schedule and the State
> Chose for eugenic reasons who should mate
> With whom, and when. Each idle song and dance
> Was fixed by law and nothing left to chance.

In this earthly paradise, which remarkably foreshadows Aldous Huxley's *Brave New World*, Dymer meekly endures

[1] *Dymer*, E. P. Dutton & Co., New York, 1926, p. 2. By permission of the publishers. Published in England by J. M. Dent & Sons.

the trained attention of his supervisors until one April morning, at the age of nineteen, he lands a good blow on his teacher's head (instantly killing him) and joyfully flees to the forest. There he comes upon a magical castle, in a dark room of which he lies down on "a knee-depth of warm pillows on the ground" [2] and passes a passionate night with the mysterious girl whom he discovers beside him in the darkness.

The aftermath is as unpleasant as that suffered some years later by John of Puritania in *The Pilgrim's Regress* when he becomes involved with brown girls. Dymer, seeking his beloved of the night before, is stopped at every door by an abominably hideous old hag. Revolted and frustrated, he leaves the castle and wanders into the woods.

There he encounters a man whose arms and legs have been hacked off. The poor devil, painfully bleeding to death, explains that this was the doing of Bran—a red-haired rabble-rouser who had taken advantage of Dymer's dramatic rebellion to lead a general insurrection against the established order. Murder and arson are now the normal pattern of life. The dying man has been punished because Bran suspected him of luke-warmness in the general game of massacre.

In despair, the hero dozes off and has a sort of pantheistic, almost Wordsworthian vision. When he awakes he enters an old house where lives an aged magician. The latter offers him the magic aid of dreams, and Dymer accepts. In his dream he encounters the girl with whom he had shared the same dark night. As he afterwards recounted to his host— [3]

[2] *Ibid.*, p. 22. By permission of the publishers.
[3] *Ibid.*, p. 80. By permission of the publishers.

"She said, for this land only did men love
The shadow-lands of earth. All our disease
Of longing, all the hopes we fabled of,
Fortunate islands or Hesperean seas
Or woods beyond the West, were but the breeze
That blew from off those shores: one farspent breath
That reached even to the world of change and death.

"She told me I had journeyed home at last
Into the golden age and the good countrie
That had been always there. She made me cast
My cares behind forever:—on her knee
Worshipped me, lord and love—oh, I can see
Her red lips even now! Is it not wrong
That men's delusions should be made so strong?"

However, the girl was only a projection of himself. In his vision the fool's paradise had quickly faded, leaving King Lust; a swarm of shaggy satyrs had begun beating tom-toms and gamboling in an obscene dance.

The magician, angered that Dymer is no longer willing to accept the aid of black magic, tells him to run. Dymer does so, barely in time to escape the bullet aimed at him.

The conclusion of the poem is not too clear, though presumably symbolizing spiritual rebirth. Dymer finds that his union with the girl has spawned a monster which flits about wreaking great harm on men. In penitence he ascends into the air to battle his offspring. He is slain in the conflict, but comes back to life— [4]

A wing'd and sworded shape, through whom the air
Poured as through glass: and its foam-tumbled hair

[4] *Ibid.*, p. 105. By permission of the publishers.

Lay white about the shoulders and the whole
Pure body brimmed with life, as a full bowl.

The entire poem displays an appealing "pre-Christian" idealism combined with burgeoning gifts of satire, but its value as pure poetry is slight.

Apart from the two volumes of poetry, Lewis—following in the tradition of Macdonald—has interwoven verse in two of his books—*The Pilgrim's Regress* and *The Great Divorce.* In the latter the Bright Spirits—welcoming one of the saved—sing a hymn modeled on the parallelism of the Hebrew psalms. It contains reasonably effective lines such as—[5]

The Happy Trinity is her home: nothing can trouble her joy.
She is the bird that evades every net: the wild deer that leaps every pitfall.
Like the mother bird to its chickens or a shield to the arm'd knight: so is the Lord to her mind, in His unchanging lucidity.

and other lines as unsuccessfully down-to-earth as—[6]

Bogies will not scare her in the dark: bullets will not frighten her in the day.

and—

They take her hand at hard places: she will not stub her toes in the dark.

The verses in *The Pilgrim's Regress* are more numerous and show considerable technical variety. Only one of them,

[5] *The Great Divorce,* p. 122.
[6] *Ibid.,* p. 123.

I confess, lingers strongly enough in my mind to be singled out for quotation here. It is the song of the Northern Dragon. A couple of its stanzas have a quaint and pleasing pathos: [7]

"Now I keep watch on the gold in my rock cave
In a country of stones: old, deplorable dragon,
Watching my hoard. In winter night the gold
Freezes through toughest scales my cold belly.
The jagged crowns and twisted cruel rings
Knobbly and icy are old dragon's bed.

"Often I wish I hadn't eaten my wife,
Though worm grows not to dragon till he eat worm.
She could have helped me, watch and watch about,
Guarding the hoard. Gold would have been the safer.
I could uncoil my weariness at times and take
A little sleep, sometimes when she was watching.

Lewis still writes occasional poems. Some of them have appeared in *The Spectator* and other magazines. Recently most have been published in *Punch* under the initials, "N. W." ("*Punch* is the only place left where poetry that depends on clever rhyme schemes is welcome," Lewis says.)

It is clear that Lewis has never completely found himself as a poet. He has experimented with alliterative verse, free verse, parallelism, and elaborate stanzaic patterns, but somehow his poetry has not shaken down into an individual style. One can seldom read a prose book of his without feeling that no other person could have written it; his poetry

[7] *The Pilgrim's Regress*, Sheed and Ward, Inc., New York, 1944, p. 248. By permission of the publishers.

seems to have been composed by half a dozen men, none having the talent of C. S. Lewis. Almost everything that he has said in verse he has said better in prose.

He abandoned poetry as his main medium at about the time he was approaching intellectual and literary maturity. What would have happened if he had not done so is one of the futile "might-have-been's" of literary history. His writing is so packed with ideas that only the ability of a Dante or a T. S. Eliot could handle them in verse. One must assume that Lewis wisely reconciled himself to his inherent limitations as a poet, and chose to say extremely well in prose what he could only stammer in verse.

The one poetic genre in which he excels is adult nonsense verse. Here he rivals Lewis Carroll. It is regrettable that he has not written more of his delightful jingles, and that to locate the few in print requires a painful search through magazine files. As an example of one of his few completely successful poems I cite, in its entirety, "Awake, My Lute!": [8]

I stood in the gloom of a spacious room
    Where I listened for hours (on and off)
To a terrible bore with a beard like a snore
    And a heavy rectangular cough,
Who discoursed on the habits of orchids and rabbits
    And how an electron behaves
And a way to cure croup with solidified soup
    In a pattern of circular waves;
Till I suddenly spied that what stood at his side
    Was a richly upholstered baboon
With paws like the puns in a poem of Donne's

[8] *The Atlantic Monthly,* November 1943, pp. 113 and 115. Quoted by permission of the publishers.

And a tail like a voyage to the Moon.
Then I whispered, "Look out! For I very much doubt
If your colleague is really a man."
But the lecturer said, without turning his head,
"Oh, that's only the Beverage Plan!"
As one might have foreseen, the whole sky became green
At this most injudicious remark,
For the Flood had begun and we both had to run
For our place in the queue to the Ark.
Then, I hardly know how (we were swimming by now),
The sea got all covered with scum
Made of publishers' blurbs and irregular verbs
Of the kind which have datives in *-um;*
And the waves were so high that far up in the sky
We saw the grand lobster, and heard
How he snorted, "Compare the achievements of Blair
With the grave of King Alfred the Third,
And add a brief note and if possible quote,
And distinguish and trace and discuss
The probable course of a Methodist horse
When it's catching a decimal buss."
My answer was Yes. But they marked it N. S.,
And a truffle-fish grabbed at my toe,
And dragged me deep down to a bombulous town
Where the traffic was silent and slow.
Then a voice out of heaven observed, "Quarter past seven!"
And I threw all the waves off my head,
For that voice beyond doubt was the voice of my scout,
And the bed of that sea was my bed.

8. The Scholar

If C. S. Lewis is a second-rate poet, his keenest enemies grant that he is a first-rate critic and scholar. Of the five books that belong here, the longest and most important is *The Allegory of Love.*

The work is an essay in social history and at the same time a treatment of the evolution of a particular literary genre. The social history has to do with the astonishing rise and development of "courtly love," which sprang up almost full-blown in Southern France during the eleventh century and quickly spread into other parts of Western Europe. Courtly love was a highly stylized form of romantic love, the goal being adultery not marriage. As such, it formed a world apart from Christian morality and sometimes became almost a rival religion. But adulterous though it was, it introduced a tenderness and consideration into the relations of men and women which had been conspicuously lacking from the ancient idea of marriage.

The literary genre studied by Lewis is the allegory. He traces it back to late Roman times, and shows how it became the favorite form for writing about courtly love. In a succession of brilliantly written sections he brings to life such writers as Ovid, Chrétien de Troyes, Andreas Capellanus, Guillaume de Lorris, Jean de Meung, Chaucer, and Spenser, with passing attention to many less known figures.

The book culminates in the treatment of Spenser, for

with him the English allegory reaches its fullest development, and at the same time the ideal of courtly love definitely emerges from its adulterous associations and passes into marriage. Modern romantic love, with marriage as its normal goal, has become a part of the social pattern; Christianity and the religion of love have made peace.

The attempt to juggle social history and simultaneously follow the growth of a literary type produces a seesawing effect at times, though this was scarcely to be avoided. Some critics contend—perhaps rightly—that the section on Spenser is so detailed that all the earlier part of the book seems a long introduction to an analysis of *The Faerie Queene*. However, one can scarcely regret the attention paid to Spenser. Lewis threads his way with ease through the great allegory, and the book is justified by the value of this chapter alone.

The other four books attempt less and possess varying degrees of unity. *Rehabilitations* is a series of essays, based mostly on addresses delivered at various times. The majority of them are defenses of someone or something recently under attack.

For example, Lewis defends Shelley from T. S. Eliot's strictures by taking Eliot's own "classical" standards and using them to vindicate Shelley and attack Eliot's hero, Dryden. In another essay Lewis praises one of his favorite authors, William Morris, for the paradoxical reason that Morris's statement of Pagan experience is "chemically pure," and represents a kind of rock-bottom reality on which both pagans and Christians can build: [1]

[1] *Rehabilitations and Other Essays*, Oxford University Press, London, New York, Toronto, 1939, pp. 54–55. By permission of the publishers.

> For Morris has 'faced the facts.' This is the paradox of him. He seems to retire far from the real world and to build a world out of his wishes; but when he has finished the result stands out as a picture of experience ineluctably true. No full-grown mind wants optimism or pessimism—philosophies of the nursery where they are not philosophies of the clinic; but to have presented in one vision the ravishing sweetness and the heart-breaking melancholy of our experience, to have shown how the one continually passes over into the other, and to have combined all this with a stirring practical creed, this is to have presented the *datum* which all our adventures, worldly and other-worldly alike, must take into account. There are many writers greater than Morris. You can go on from him to all sorts of subtleties, delicacies, and sublimities which he lacks. But you can hardly go behind him.

One of the essays deplores the distinction between high- and low-brow literature and contends that the labels blur the purposes of true criticism; that instead of pigeon-holing a given book the critic should look for specific excellencies and shortcomings.

Of the three essays not intended to "rehabilitate," the one entitled "Bluspels and Flanansferes" deals with a problem much debated by the semanticists: whether metaphorical language is an enemy to truth and clear thinking. Lewis advocates a generous use of metaphor, adding only that it should be *consciously* employed and not mistaken for literal statement: [2]

> To speak more plainly, he who would increase the meaning and decrease the meaningless verbiage in his own

[2] *Ibid.*, pp. 154 and 156. By permission of the publishers.

> speech and writing, must do two things. He must become conscious of the fossilized metaphors in his words; and he must freely use new metaphors, which he creates for himself. . . . The second is perhaps the more important of the two: we are never less the slaves of metaphor than when we are making metaphor, or hearing it new made. . . .
>
> . . . The percentage of mere syntax masquerading as meaning may vary from something like 100 per cent. in political writers, journalists, psychologists, and economists, to something like forty per cent. in the writers of children's stories. . . .

The concluding essay, "Christianity and Literature," points out the clash in atmosphere between modern criticism, with its emphasis on originality and spontaneity, and the New Testament stress on imitation as the way to perfection. Lewis argues that to the Christian his own experience as mere fact is of no great importance; at most it is the medium through which he perceives something universally profitable. The Christian is also inclined to take literature a trifle less heavily than does the esthetic pagan; he may appear downright frivolous.

The Personal Heresy is the outcome of an unusual collaboration between Lewis and Dr. E. M. W. Tillyard, fellow of Jesus College, Cambridge. The controversy began when Lewis published an article in *Essays and Studies* (English Association) in 1934, attacking the excessive emphasis on biographical details in criticism. Tillyard replied in the same journal, and the interchange continued until six essays had been produced, which eventually appeared in book form.

Like all arguments, this one wanders back and forth a great deal, comes to dead ends on both sides, and never fully resolves the points at issue—which seem to center at least partly around the definition of the word "personality." In general, Lewis argues for enjoying a poem or other work of imaginative literature on its own merits, without thinking too much about the author; Tillyard contends that contact with the author's personality, as revealed in his writing, is one of the main pleasures of reading. Both contributors write with courtliness and express relish for intelligent opposition. The semantic difficulties are never completely overcome, and though many interesting things are touched upon in the jousting I would call the tournament a draw.

A Preface to Paradise Lost ranks next after the *Allegory* as Lewis's most sustained piece of criticism. Based on the Ballard Matthews Lectures which he delivered in 1941 at University College, North Wales, the book is prefaced with a dedication to Charles Williams, to whom Lewis attributes the rediscovery of a true tradition of Miltonic criticism after more than a century of misunderstanding.[3]

A series of chapters on the epic form are followed by a detailed treatment of the principal stumbling blocks to enjoyment of *Paradise Lost.* To defend the epic Lewis is obliged to explain a number of concepts now grown obscure or unpopular: notably that of "hierarchy" as opposed to modern equalitarianism. Most of all, he rescues Milton from the dubious compliment bestowed upon him by the Romantic critics: that the Devil is the real hero of *Paradise*

[3] Lewis is referring to Williams' preface to *The Poetical Works of Milton,* The World's Classics, 1940.

Lost. To Lewis, Milton builds Satan up in order to knock him down—[4]

> From hero to general, from general to politician, from politician to secret service agent, and thence to a thing that peers in at bedroom or bathroom windows, and thence to a toad, and finally to a snake—such is the progress of Satan.

This point, I think, is well proved, and should lay the ghost of much Miltonic criticism. Another contention of Lewis's is more dubious—his belief that, with the exception of one or two minor heresies, *Paradise Lost* conforms to the theology of classical Christianity. Lewis admits that in Milton's other writings there is clear evidence of his Arianism—he believed that God the Son was not preëxistent with God the Father—but argues that *Paradise Lost* does not clearly imply this or any other major heresy. The question is too complicated to thresh out here; I can only say that I, like some others who have examined the book, am not wholly convinced.

In any event, the work is very *usable*. The English professor in me sees where it could serve a double purpose in literature courses: it is at once an introduction to the epic in general, and an admirable handbook to help students overcome their initial terror when facing *Paradise Lost*.

Lewis's most recent work of scholarship is also a last tribute to his deceased friend, Charles Williams. *Arthurian Torso* is divided into two parts. The first half is the posthumous fragment, *The Figure of Arthur* (Williams' study of the development and significance of the Arthurian

[4] *A Preface to Paradise Lost*, Oxford University Press, London, New York, Toronto, 1942, p. 97. By permission of the publishers.

legends), edited by Lewis. In the second part of the volume Lewis provides a highly useful commentary on Williams' profound but extremely difficult poetry dealing with Arthurian themes (*Taliessin through Logres* and *The Region of the Summer Stars*). If, as seems likely, Williams' full stature is yet to be realized by the general public, his friend's essay is likely to be of crucial importance, since no one is in a better position to help the reader over the difficult places in Williams' Arthuriad.

Lewis's other scholarly writings are found mostly in journals and magazines; one or two have appeared in pamphlet form or as a contribution to compositely written books. If my study were intended mainly for literary specialists I should have to analyze all these in detail, but since I am primarily concerned with Lewis the theologian, philosopher, and creative writer, I shall omit them.

Taking the man's scholarship as a whole, several characteristics are evident: (1) His immense reading in classical antiquity and the medieval literature of Western Europe makes him an unusually sure guide in literary problems having ancient roots. (2)His critical approach is to concentrate on the work itself, and to subordinate the personal minutiæ of the authors' lives. He does not shun the "Historical Method" altogether, but he never carries it to the extreme desired by Screwtape. Though Lewis recognizes that any work of literature is partially shaped by history and social conditions, his main object is to discover wisdom and delight in books of all periods rather than to establish "who influenced the ancient writer, and how far the statement is consistent with what he said in other books," [5] etc., etc. (3) Throughout his criticism he wages an off-and-on

[5] *The Screwtape Letters*, pp. 139–140.

war against the "sub-Romantics" and "counter-Romantics." The former—the worshippers of instinct, life force, etc.—he treats with tolerant contempt. His greatest irritation is reserved for the counter-Romantics, notably T. S. Eliot. He never completely loses his urbanity but enough heat seeps into his words to suggest that what appears on the printed page is a pale echo of the thoughts in the author's mind. Lewis's quarrel with Eliot seems to be essentially that Eliot is too high-brow and esoteric in his criticism. Lewis, who reads pulp fiction as well as the *Aeneid,* and apologizes for neither, defends what might be called a middle-brow approach, and opposes Eliot's apparent attempt to make the appreciation of literature the priestly task of a small élite. Here, as in his attitude toward Christianity, Lewis insists that two feet on the ground are the *sine qua non* for getting somewhere.

9. "Mere Christianity"

> *Measured against the ages "mere Christianity" turns out to be no insipid interdenominational transparency, but something positive, self-consistent, and inexhaustible. I know it, indeed, to my cost. In the days when I still hated Christianity, I learned to recognize, like some all too familiar smell, that almost unvarying* something *which met me, now in Puritan Bunyan, now in Anglican Hooker, now in Thomist Dante.*
>
> —Introduction to *The Incarnation of the Word of God,* p. 8.*

Most of Lewis's books, as we have seen, are direct or indirect defenses of Christianity, and in them he proves himself a multiple-threat champion. For the reader who wants a simple, logical presentation of the faith he offers the broadcast talks. To ease the potential convert over two major obstacles there are *The Problem of Pain* and *Miracles.* For those who are impatient of formal logic but susceptible to the oblique approach he provides philosophic scientifiction. *The Screwtape Letters* are aimed at any chinks in the armor of resolute skeptics; more than one staunch atheist has first admired the *Letters* as satire and then found himself troubled with previously unasked questions. And in *The Great Divorce* the waverer is told to make up his mind.

The man is a missionary—but for what kind of Christianity? Not since the first couple of centuries of the Christian era, when mutually contradictory heresies filled the air, has the word "Christian" been so elastic as it is today. It means everything from "believing the Bible from cover to cover" to possessing a vague feeling of benevolence toward "neighbors" who live in such remote parts of the world that no practical obligations are entailed.

In a rough and ready way, there are three main types of twentieth-century Christianity, with countless shadings in between. This classification is based not on fashions in vestments but on theology. There is Fundamentalist Christianity, Modernist Christianity, and something that for want of a better label I shall call Classical Christianity.

In its most extreme forms, Fundamentalism believes that God created the earth approximately 4004 B.C., and extracted Adam's rib to make Eve; the doctrine of evolution is denied or viewed with black suspicion. Along with a very literal interpretation of the Bible goes a steadfast faith in the traditional dogmas of Christianity: the divinity of Christ, the Atonement, Heaven, Hell, Original Sin, and all the rest.

Fundamentalism is popularly associated with certain Protestant churches (and is more prevalent in America than Europe), but as a matter of fact, Roman Catholic scholarship, since the suppression of the Modernist heresy in the Roman Church around the turn of the century, has often bent over backward in a semi-Fundamentalist direction. However, it has never reached the extreme position of some of the Protestant Fundamentalists.

At the opposite end of the spectrum are the all-out Modernists, who regard Christianity as a system of ethics or program for social reform. Their theology, when they have any, is deliberately vague. Christ is not God incarnate, but a great moral teacher; Heaven and Hell are psychological states; Original Sin, if admitted into the system, is simply another name for "cultural lag." God sometimes hovers benevolently in the background; at other times He seems little more than a shorthand symbol for social advancement.

Such are the two extremes. Fundamentalism invites a conflict between religion and science (many of the most confirmed atheists I have known were reared as sturdy Fundamentalists and then studied geology or biology); Modernism resolves the supposed conflict by making religion so vague that it won't get in the way.

The third position, being less dramatic, is harder to define. "Classical Christianity" is based on a handful of doctrines which are stated or implied in the New Testament and are conveniently summarized in the Apostles' Creed and Nicene Creed. The starting point is the complete objective reality of God, who is the Creator of the universe and the source of all meaningful reality. God is revealed in what is technically called three "Persons"—the Father, the Son, and the Holy Ghost. The supreme event of history is the birth, life, death, resurrection, and ascension of Jesus—the second Person of the Trinity. By this historical event, the alienation of man from God (which dates back to the "Fall") is ended, at least "in principle," and a new relationship established. But the final decision is still up to the individual: each person, by his own choices, destines himself for an eternity in Heaven or Hell.

This thumb-nail sketch of Classical Christianity may

suggest that it differs little from Fundamentalism. Actually, it *is* closer to Fundamentalism than to Modernism, but there are significant differences, especially in the intellectual climate that the two engender. These divergences come out particularly in the way the Bible is regarded. To the extreme Fundamentalist, it is almost a laboratory manual. To the believer in Classical Christianity, the Bible (more especially the Old Testament) is not so much a universal encyclopedia as the work of dozens of men responding as best they could to divine inspiration. Some episodes are not necessarily meant to be taken literally: it is of no importance whether Eve literally ate an apple or whether God created the earth in seven days of twenty-four hours each—the important thing is that the Adam-and-Eve story symbolizes the Fall of man from a state of original harmony with God, and the Creation story means that but for God there would be no universe.

The "conflict between science and religion" is a much more agonizing problem for the Fundamentalist than for the Classical Christian. The former often erects barricades against the findings of the laboratory; the latter tries to integrate them into the broad, inclusive framework of Christian theology.

What I have styled "Classical Christianity" is much the same thing as Lewis's "mere Christianity" or "plain, central Christianity." A careful reading of Lewis's books leaves the conviction that he is squarely in the middle of the Christian tradition: an uncompromising defender of the doctrines telescoped into the Creeds, but chary of excessive Bibliolatry. If occasionally he leans to one side or the other, it is perhaps more often in a slightly Fundamentalist direction.

In *The Case for Christianity* Lewis pays his brief respects to "Christianity-and-water," which is his curt description of Modernism: [1]

> Very well then, atheism is too simple. And I'll tell you another view that is also too simple. It's the view I call Christianity-and-water, the view that just says there's a good God in Heaven and everything is all right—leaving out all the difficult and terrible doctrines about sin and hell and the devil, and the redemption. Both these are boys' philosophies.
>
> It is no good asking for a simple religion. After all, real things *aren't* simple. They *look* simple, but they're not.

Mr. Broad, in *The Pilgrim's Regress,* is of remarkably little assistance to John the pilgrim. John wants answers to specific questions; Mr. Broad, with the fond smile of greater maturity, tells him that [2] "one loses faith in abstract logic as one grows older. Do you never feel that the truth is so great and so simple that no mere words can contain it?" John asks how to reach the Island of his dreams; Mr. Broad urges him to study botany: [3] "It would open a new world to you." And he adds, "A new window on the Infinite."

Mr. Broad reappears in *The Great Divorce* wearing gaiters. The apostate bishop, when urged to remain in Heaven, decides that Duty demands his return to Hell (only he doesn't know it is Hell): [4]

> Bless my soul, I'd nearly forgotten. Of course I can't come with you. I have to be back next Friday to read a

[1] P. 35.

[2] *The Pilgrim's Regress,* Sheed and Ward Inc., New York, 1944, p. 148. By permission of the publishers.

[3] *Ibid.,* p. 149. By permission of the publishers.

[4] Pp. 39–40.

> paper. We have a little Theological Society down there. . . . I'm taking the text about growing up to the measure of the stature of Christ and working out an idea which I feel sure you'll be interested in. I'm going to point out how people always forget that Jesus (here the Ghost bowed) was a comparatively young man when he died. He would have outgrown some of his earlier views, you know, if he'd lived. As he might have done, with a little more tact and patience. I am going to ask my audience to consider what his mature views would have been. A profoundly interesting question. What a different Christianity we might have had if only the Founder had reached his full stature! I shall end up by pointing out how this deepens the significance of the Crucifixion.

And thereupon, nodding its head and beaming with a bright clerical smile, the Ghost departs for Hell, humming softly to itself, "City of God, how broad and far." The portrait of the bishop, sharply etched with the author's malice, is one of Lewis's most successful satirical sketches.

It would be possible to make a long list of passages in other books to show the jabs that Lewis takes at Modernist Christianity. Evidently many Modernists have crossed his path and irritated him by what he considers their intellectual fuzziness and refusal to face basic decisions—such as the question of whether the Supernatural does in fact exist. I suspect that Lewis has had less contact with Fundamentalists. Nowhere, so far as I know, does he pen a portrait of a snake cultist or satirize the sort of revivalists who held forth in Dayton, Tennessee, during the Scopes Monkey Trial. His points of divergence from Fundamentalism come out more quietly—for example, in *Miracles* his willingness to regard some of the miracles of the Old Testament as [5] "mythology chosen by God to be the vehicle of the earliest sacred truths" and his description of the Genesis story of Creation as being told [6] "in the form of a folk tale."

Lewis's theology begins with a conviction both passionate and intellectual that God exists. No Mohammedan, sensing the omnipotence of Allah above the burning desert, could express the final fact with more intensity: [7] "Let us dare to say that God is a particular Thing. Once He was the only Thing: but He is creative, He made other things to be."

Although a Trinitarian, Lewis says comparatively little about the Third Person of the Trinity. In a conversation with my friend, Professor David W. Soper, Lewis once explained that he regards the Holy Ghost as being, so to speak, God within us; His principal mission is to lead us to Christ. For this reason, the Third Person is singularly elusive when a prosaic description of the Trinity is attempted.

Lewis's theology is highly Christocentric, and his Christ is not merely a good man. *The Case for Christianity* uses St. Augustine's argument, "either God or not a good man": [8]

> A man who was merely a man and said the sort of things Jesus said wouldn't be a great moral teacher. He'd either be a lunatic—on a level with the man who says he's a poached egg—or else he'd be the Devil of Hell. You must make your choice. Either this man was, and is, the Son of

[5] P. 161 n.
[6] P. 42.
[7] P. 106.
[8] P. 45.

> God: or else a madman or something worse. You can shut Him up for a fool, you can spit at Him and kill Him as a demon; or you can fall at His feet and call Him Lord and God. But don't let us come with any patronising nonsense about His being a great human teacher. He hasn't left that open to us. He didn't intend to.

Constantly throughout his books Lewis stresses the complete divinity of Christ, as well as his humanity. In the interplanetary novels we see the Malacandrians and Perelandrians worshipping Maleldil, who is none other than Christ. In *Perelandra* Ransom, trying to summon up his courage for a physical combat with the Un-man, hears the voice of the unseen Maleldil: [9] "It is not for nothing that you are named Ransom. . . . My name also is Ransom."

This brings up a second point. Not only does Lewis continually emphasize the divinity of Christ, but he goes to great pains to picture Christ's primary mission as one of Atonement. It is true that Lewis does not commit himself to one particular theory of how the Atonement works (this distressed the Roman Catholic priest who read the original draft of *The Case for Christianity*), but he makes it very clear that Christ did something more than "setting a good example" when He suffered death upon the cross. The best idea of Lewis's own position, though he presents it very tentatively, is found in *The Case for Christianity:* [10]

> But supposing God became a man—suppose our human nature which can suffer and die was amalgamated with

[9] From *Perelandra*, pp. 153–154. Copyright, 1944 by Clive Staples Lewis. Used by permission of The Macmillan Company. Published in England by John Lane.

[10] P. 50.

> God's nature in one person—then that person could help us. He could surrender His will, and suffer and die, because He was man; and He could do it perfectly because He was God. You and I can go through this process only if God does it in us; but God can do it only if He becomes man. Our attempts at this dying will succeed only if we men share in God's dying, just as our thinking can succeed only because it is a drop out of the ocean of His intelligence: but we can't share God's dying unless God dies; and He can't die except by being a man. That is the sense in which He pays our debt, and suffers for us what He Himself needn't suffer at all.

Lewis's belief in the divinity of Christ—and particularly the central place he gives to the Atonement—runs counter not only to popular naturalism but to many modern varieties of Christianity. But he does not stop there. He embraces and defends other doctrines still more repugnant to the intellectual climate of the times. These require detailed treatment by themselves.

10. Unpopular Doctrines

> *Of course, I quite agree that the Christian religion is, in the long run, a thing of unspeakable comfort. But it doesn't begin in comfort; it begins in the dismay I've been describing, and it's just no good trying to go on to that comfort without first going through that dismay.*
>
> —*The Case for Christianity,* pp. 27–28.

Progress and the goodness of human nature—until very recently they were taken for granted in most of modern thought. These assumptions contradict what the main tradition of Christianity has always said. Christianity is wildly optimistic and bleakly pessimistic at the same time. It leads its followers to sing joyful hymns at the thought of the glorious destiny offered them through no merit of their own, but it is darkly skeptical about the actual state of man when left in the raw state. Like a ruthless doctor, it begins with a diagnosis of deep-seated disease before it talks of remedies and the recovery of radiant health.

It is Lewis's repeated insistence on the diagnostic side of Christianity that sets him most violently in opposition to the spirit of the age. "Christ takes it for granted that men are bad," he writes in *The Problem of Pain.*[1] "Until we really feel this assumption of His to be true, though we are part of the world He came to save, we are not part of the

[1] P. 45.

audience to whom His words are addressed. We lack the first condition for understanding what He is talking about."

To explain how creatures made by God have turned into sinful rebels Lewis relies on the ancient tale of Adam and Eve. Their fatal revolt is symbolized in *The Pilgrim's Regress* by *Peccatum Adae*—a canyon so steep and wide that the pilgrim can reach the further side only by the supernatural aid of Mother Kirk. *The Problem of Pain* is almost Fundamentalist in its interpretation of the story of the Fall: [2]

> We do not know how many of these creatures [men] God made, nor how long they continued in the Paradisal state. But sooner or later they fell. Someone or something whispered that they could become as gods—that they could cease directing their lives to their Creator. . . . They wanted, as we say, to "call their souls their own." . . . We have no idea in what particular act, or series of acts, the self-contradictory, impossible wish found expression. For all I can see, it might have concerned the literal eating of a fruit, but the question is of no consequence.

Whatever the exact particulars of the ancient revolt, its consequences continue in full force, setting each man at war with God.

The "someone or something," whispering to the earliest men, is unmistakably the Devil. "I know someone will ask me, 'Do you really mean, at this time of day, to re-introduce our old friend the devil—hoofs and horns and all?' " Lewis says in *The Case for Christianity*,[3] "Well, what the time of day has to do with it I don't know. And I'm not particular

[2] Pp. 67–68.
[3] P. 40.

about the hoofs and horns. But in other respects my answer is, 'Yes, I do.' "

The Screwtape Letters imaginatively depict the "Lowerarchy" of Hell, with its lord the Devil and its vast bureaucracy of demons, some of whom are sent to the earth to tempt individual persons or to launch intellectual and emotional trends favorable to the purposes of Hell. Screwtape (who is not Satan but a high official in the demonic society) is a very shrewd psychologist, with an alarming ability to detect the tiniest defect in each person's moral armor. The philosophy of Hell and that of the Enemy (= God) are thus contrasted: [4]

> We want cattle who can finally become food; He wants servants who can finally become sons. We want to suck in, He wants to give out. We are empty and would be filled; He is full and flows over. Our war aim is a world in which Our Father Below has drawn all other beings into himself: the Enemy wants a world full of beings united to Him but still distinct.

Screwtape has a certain dash and charm. Future critics are certain to insist that Lewis secretly sided with him, because His Infernal Excellency is so much more vivid than the pallid Christian hero of the book. But I am sure they will be mistaken. A truer picture of how Lewis looks upon the Devil is to be found in *Perelandra*—a book with less brilliance but more sensitivity and depth than the celebrated *Letters*.

In *Perelandra,* as we have seen, Weston becomes more and more an empty shell housing the incarnate Devil, until Lewis refers to him simply as the Un-man. In verbal debate

[4] P. 46.

the Un-man is more than a match for Ransom as they battle for the soul of the green woman. But his intellect is nothing but a tool, arguments merely a means toward an end and never a quest for truth. In his moments of leisure he does not read Plato nor even the Marquis de Sade: he passes the time by ripping the skin off frogs' backs. When Ransom surprised him—[5]

> It looked at Ransom in silence and at last began to smile. We have all often spoken—Ransom himself had often spoken—of a devilish smile. Now he realised that he had never taken the words seriously. The smile was not bitter, nor raging, nor, in an ordinary sense, sinister; it was not even mocking. It seemed to summon Ransom, with a horrible naïveté of welcome, into the world of its own pleasures, as if all men were at one in those pleasures. . . . This creature was whole-hearted. The extremity of its evil had passed beyond all struggle into some state which bore a horrible similarity to innocence. It was beyond vice as the Lady was beyond virtue.

Perelandra is a myth, not a treatise on dogmatic theology. But the impression gained from the Un-man is that Lewis regards the Devil as a being with tremendously clever brains, perverted to completely evil purposes; terrifyingly shrewd as to means, completely obtuse about the ends of the universe.

In any case, these two unpopular doctrines add up to this: The Fall of Man has left everyone with the taint of Original Sin, so that he is in need of more than human help; at the same time, the Devil and his sub-devils are the real rulers of the earth, and our poor planet is the scene of a

[5] P. 113.

cosmic struggle between the dominant forces of darkness and the struggling forces of good.

The latter invaded the occupied planet most dramatically when Christ appeared—[6] "Christianity is the story of how the rightful king has landed, you might say landed in disguise, and is calling us all to take part in a great campaign of sabotage." If man leans toward evil and the powers of Hell are ever at his elbow to encourage the leaning, the significance of the Atonement becomes sharper. It was the radical remedy that God undertook, at His own cost, to rescue mankind from the trap into which it had blithely fallen.

However, all talk of "Atonement" and "rescue" means little, if, at the end of sixty or seventy years, the individual ceases to exist. Christianity presupposes immortality.

Immortality and its fearful consequences loom large in Lewis's books. He believes in the existence of Heaven and Hell, and believes that each person in the long run will arrive in one place or the other—and stay there.

It may seem odd that I am including Heaven among the unpopular doctrines, but I think the inclusion can be justified. The modern objection to belief in Heaven is that it is a will o' the wisp: the man who daydreams about heavenly mansions does not spend sufficient time organizing slum clearance projects. The feeling has grown up that to speculate about what may lie beyond the embalmer's table is anti-social.

Lewis's argument is simply that either Heaven exists or it does not. If it does exist, the fact is of paramount importance and must be faced, regardless of whether it is useful at political get-togethers.

[6] *The Case for Christianity*, p. 40.

His most thorough treatment of the subject is contained in Chapter X of *The Problem of Pain.*. Here he imagines Heaven as a place or state in which each individual is constantly surrendering himself to God—but at the same time becoming more distinct, acquiring a more individual "personality," than he had on earth. This double process constitutes Heaven. Lewis likens it to a dance— [7] "As we draw nearer to its uncreated rhythm, pain and pleasure sink almost out of sight. There is joy in the dance, but it does not exist for the sake of joy. It does not even exist for the sake of good, or of love. It is Love Himself, and Good Himself, and therefore happy. It does not exist for us, but we for it."

All this is indirect, metaphorical language. In *The Great Divorce* Lewis becomes almost as symbolical as the Book of Revelation. Like St. John, he hints at the ineffable by concrete pictures, but—perhaps forewarned by the literal interpretation many devout Christians have fastened on Revelation—he warns the reader that everything he describes is a dream, not a Baedeker of Heaven.

The ghosts that drift through the dream are scarcely more visible than thin smoke. The diamond-hard grass of Heaven can be seen through their feet, and is unbearably painful to them (only if they surrender themselves utterly can they "thicken up" and tread confidently across the meadows). The Bright People, by contrast, seem more solid than life. The landscape is beautiful and titanic—a terror to ghosts and a delight to the saved.

When he deals with Hell in *The Problem of Pain* Lewis confesses that he shares the emotional revulsion of his readers: [8] "We are told that it is a detestable doctrine—

[7] P. 141.
[8] P. 107.

and indeed, I too detest it from the bottom of my heart." He would gladly amputate the doctrine from Christianity but cannot; it has the support of Christ's own words, has always been held by Christendom, and is supported by reason: [9] "If a game is played, it must be possible to lose it."

The "game" is self-surrender. It has to be voluntary. But if Free Will really exists, it must exist for all eternity: the individual must forever remain free to say Yes or No to God; otherwise Free Will is merely a temporary concession. Such is the logical impasse of the theologian.

The most tormenting problem of the orthodox Christian is to reconcile the love of God and the reality of Hell. Lewis puts it in all its starkness: [10]

> The problem is not simply that of a God who consigns some of His creatures to final ruin. That would be the problem if we were Mahometans. Christianity, true, as always, to the complexity of the real, presents us with something knottier and more ambiguous—a God so full of mercy that He becomes man and dies by torture to avert that final ruin from His creatures, and who yet, where that heroic remedy fails, seems unwilling, or even unable, to arrest the ruin by an act of mere power.

His books at times seem to show a slight wavering in his attitude toward Hell—not that he ever doubts its existence, but he has not fully made up his mind whether it is a state of retribution or simply what the wicked create for themselves. (The final result, as Lewis points out, is the same in either case.)

The angelic Guide in *The Pilgrim's Regress* views "the

[9] P. 106.
[10] Pp. 107–108.

Black Hole" as God's last mercy to lost souls who will accept no other favor: a means of halting what would otherwise be the endless propagation of evil—[11] "The walls of the black hole are the tourniquet on the wound through which the lost soul else would bleed to a death she never reached. It is the Landlord's last service to those who will let him do nothing better for them."

The Problem of Pain grapples directly, if reluctantly, with the idea of retribution. Lewis pens a character sketch of a man who has led a completely self-centered, double-crossing life—but also a highly successful one—and asks: [12] "Can you really desire that such a man, *remaining what he is* (and he must be able to do that if he has free will) should be confirmed forever in his present happiness—should continue, for all eternity, to be perfectly convinced that the laugh is on his side?" He then goes on to say that he has described the theory of retribution first because it is the most repellent one, but that any Christian is at liberty to regard Hell not as a sentence imposed on an evil man but as [13] "the mere fact of being what he is . . . to live wholly in the self and to make the best of what he finds there. And what he finds there is Hell."

It is this latter view which is developed with remarkable poignancy in *The Great Divorce.* Any of the ghosts in the gray town are at liberty to take the bus to Heaven and remain there, but to remain is a physical impossibility unless they surrender their souls to God and "thicken up." As the George Macdonald of the fantasy says,[14] "There are

[11] *The Pilgrim's Regress,* Sheed and Ward Inc., New York, 1944, p. 233. By permission of the publishers.

[12] P. 109.

[13] P. 111.

[14] P. 69.

only two kinds of people in the end: those who say to God, 'Thy will be done,' and those to whom God says, in the end, '*Thy* will be done.' All that are in Hell, choose it."

If *The Great Divorce* is taken literally it suggests a belief in Purgatory as well as Heaven and Hell. The gray town is both Hell and Purgatory: Hell for those who insist on staying there, and Purgatory (in retrospect) for those who progress from it to Heaven. However, Lewis's repeated warnings against mistaking a fantasy for a treatise come to mind here, and it is very probable that he intends no more than to suggest that the final decision is actually made by each individual.

The historical Macdonald had inclined toward a belief in universal salvation, through the eventual free choice of each soul. The glorified mentor of Lewis's fable refuses a point-blank answer to Lewis's question. It is futile for a mortal to agonize over such questions, he says; time is the lens through which we perceive what reality we can, and within the framework of time there is no answer. The question can only be answered within eternity, and Lewis is not ready for that.

The realization that there are only two possible termini to human lives is strong in Lewis's thinking and comes out constantly in casual conversations. I recall once when he was with a group of his friends. The discussion turned to *The Miracle of the Bells,* which he had just read. His main quarrel with it was that "when the characters get converted it just peps them up; none of them seems to realize that he is either going to Heaven or to Hell." I think it not too far-fetched to suggest that much of the steady power of Lewis's writing comes from his constant conviction that the human drama, for each of us, can end in only two ways; every person is a battlefield of cosmic forces of good and evil, and the individual cannot evade taking sides.

In his Preface to *The Case for Christianity* Lewis explains that he had submitted the original draft of the book to clergymen of four different denominations and they had approved it with a few minor suggestions for changes. He lists the points of disagreement and continues: "Apart from those, I believe you can take what is said in the second series [of broadcast talks] as plain Christianity which no Christian disagrees with."

It depends on how the word "Christian" is defined. A believer in Classical Christianity would agree almost entirely with Lewis. A Fundamentalist would go along most of the time but would often wish that he had been more explicit on certain points, such as the inspiration of the Bible. But a Modernist would agree with him rarely and then usually only on minor details.

Evidently in his own mind Lewis ordinarily restricts the word "Christian" to those who believe in traditional Christianity. However, he does not pretend that this rather legalistic view is the only one possible. In the Preface to *Beyond Personality* he forestalls accusations of intolerance: [15]

> There is a deeper sense of the word 'Christian' in which some who hold wrong beliefs may be more Christian than some who hold the right ones. Christ, who can see into their hearts, may recognize them as His own, and more His own than many of the orthodox. Needless to say, I never dreamed of laying down who was a 'Christian' in *that* sense. It would have been the grossest impudence for me even to raise the question, for neither I nor any mortal can possibly know the answer.

[15] P. vi.

What a mortal *can* know is the professed *beliefs* of a man —his theology—and against the beliefs of the Modernists Lewis wages a war in which quarter is neither asked nor given. When he talks of Modernism he is especially critical of clergymen who go Modernist while continuing to exercise their priestly functions and receive clerical stipends. He regards them as equal to traitorous soldiers plotting to overthrow the nation from which they get their pay.

I should perhaps add that Lewis's books do not include everything that he personally believes about Christianity. He makes a conscious effort to concentrate on the beliefs that all Christians (except the Modernists) share in common, and he plays down doctrines about which there is a serious diversity of opinion among the orthodox. As one example, for an Anglican he says remarkably little about the Sacraments in his books. He explained to me that this was intentional; the Sacraments are understood variously in the different churches, and he did not want to exercise a divisive influence. For his own part, he said, he is convinced of the "real presence" of Christ in Holy Communion (though he was not prepared to accept a particular theory, such as transubstantiation, to explain the *mode* of His presence), but he had refrained from dwelling on this point because many firmly orthodox Christians do not share his belief.

Lewis has also been careful not to identify himself with any of the factions that enliven the Anglican Church. He is obviously not Broad Church, and for this reason he is often carelessly listed as an Anglo-Catholic. Perhaps "Low Church Catholic"—a label proposed by my friend, Mr. Peter Day—is as accurate as any. Lewis's orthodoxy links him with the Anglo-Catholics, but he seems to attach less weight than they to doctrines of the nature of the Church, the Apostolic Succession, ritualistic practices, and the like. He tries to avoid writing anything that would accentuate factionalism in the Church, except that he does not conceal his conviction that the Broad Churchmen are, consciously or unconsciously, apostates, whose salvation lies in "repenting and believing."

11. Myth, Fact, and Truth

> *I have the deepest respect even for Pagan myths, still more for myths in Holy Scripture.*
>
> —*The Problem of Pain,* p. 59.
>
> . . . *I find it easier to believe in a myth of gods and demons than in one of hypostatised abstract nouns. And after all, our mythology may be much nearer to literal truth than we suppose.*
>
> —*Ibid.,* pp. 123–24.

About Christianity's main articles of faith Lewis says the response must be Yes or No. Either God exists, or He does not; Christ is God, or He is not; we live forever, or we do not.

When it comes to the relationship between fact, truth, and mythology, his viewpoint is less drastic. What he implies is a subterranean connection among the three—a connection blurred in this fallen world, but which in some apocalyptic future may become obvious again. The evidence for his attitude is found mostly in the three novels, and the reader should remember that I may draw some unjustified conclusions. Much that I say is provisional, for Lewis cannot be held accountable for every word uttered by Ransom.

It appears that Lewis believes the New Testament very much as a Fundamentalist does. The Incarnation, the Resurrection, the Ascension, Christ's miracles—these he accepts as historical facts, as definite as Caesar's invasion of Gaul. At the same time, he attributes to them a "mythological" significance: [1] "Just as God is none the less God by being Man, so the Myth remains Myth even when it becomes Fact. The story of Christ demands from us, and repays, not only a religious and historical but also an imaginative response. It is directed to the child, the poet, and the savage in us as well as to the conscience and the intellect. One of its functions is to break down dividing walls."

In the same passage he parts company with the Fundamentalists by granting that large parts of the Old Testament belong to a second level—not history, but truth in mythical form on the road toward becoming historical: [2]

> My present view—which is tentative and liable to any amount of correction—would be that just as, on the factual side, a long preparation culminates in God's becoming incarnate as Man, so, on the documentary side, the truth first appears in *mythical* form and then by a long process of condensing or focussing finally becomes incarnate as History. This involves the belief that Myth in general is. . . , at its best, a real though unfocussed gleam of divine truth falling on human imagination. The Hebrews, like other peoples, had mythology: but as they were the chosen people so their mythology was the chosen mythology. . . .

The third level is pagan mythology, which Lewis regards not as complete nonsense but as a strange mixture of grossness and beauty, inanity and truth.

This friendly response to even the most primitive mythologies leads Lewis to a more kindly attitude toward other religions than was displayed by some of the early

[1] *Miracles,* p. 161 n.
[2] *Idem.*

Church fathers, who branded the mystery cults as the deceptive handiwork of Satan because their ritual and doctrines often paralleled those of Christianity. To Lewis, resemblances of this sort are not the tricks of the evil one but the outcome of a kind of natural revelation. "If you are a Christian," he says,[3] "you don't have to believe that all the other religions are simply wrong all through . . . you are free to think that all these religions, even the queerest ones, contain at least some hint of the truth."

Somehow the subject of comparative religion came up during a conversation with Lewis, and I asked him about the relation of Christianity to other religions. He replied by a neat scheme of classification, which he has evidently thought about a good deal, though I do not believe it has yet been incorporated in any of his writings. He puts religions into two main classes: (1) Paganism proper. The mythology of Paganism, Lewis has come to believe, is always a heterogeneous mixture. It embodies real messages from God intercepted at a very remote distance and serving to prepare the way for Christianity, which is the consummation of all that is best in Paganism; intermingled with flashes of divine truth are diabolical elements—cruel and obscene rites; the third ingredient is just plain human invention—people making stories. (2) Religions that have a real theology. These would include such religions as Judaism, Christianity, Hinduism, Buddhism, Mohammedanism; perhaps also Platonism and Stoicism.

Lewis suggested another classification cutting across the first one: "thick" religions and "clear" ones (as soup is thick or clear). Paganism is invariably thick—it is orgiastic, sacramental, and appeals to the emotions rather than the

[3] *The Case for Christianity*, p. 31.

intellect or conscience. The great world religions are mostly clear ones.

Of the major faiths, the clearest is Confucianism—so clear that one is uncertain whether to call it a religion or a philosophy. Lewis's point in making the classification is that a true religion ought to be both thick and clear: "God is the God of the belly as well as of the mind, of the babe as well as of the adult." As he sees it, only two religions combine thickness and clearness. They are Hinduism and Christianity (with the latter he includes Judaism for purposes of this pigeon-holing).

But Hinduism, Lewis went on to say, is really two religions. It is clear for the hermit meditating on metaphysics and thick for the peasant widow contemplating suttee. Only Christianity combines the two elements in such a fashion that everyone must accept both.When an African savage is converted to Christianity he is taught a "clear" ethic and the rudiments of a rational theology. On the other hand, Lewis pointed out to me, "When a prig like you or me accepts Christianity he is told he must rise early on Sunday morning and participate in a prehistoric blood feast."

Everyone seems to have a book in mind that he wishes Lewis would write; I should like to see him attempt a philosophy of comparative religion.

But back to myths in general—it is in the interplanetary novels—themselves part of one mighty myth—that Lewis has the most to say. When Augray the *sorn* tries to explain the nature of the *eldila* to Ransom it suddenly occurs to the space-traveler that the persistent fables of *albs, devas* and other bright, elusive creatures might have an explanation that had never occurred to the anthropologists. Voyaging back to the earth he realizes that everything he has beheld with his own eyes will sound like mythology if he recounts it to his friends. The thought strikes him that the very distinction between history and mythology is perhaps meaningless outside of the earth.

While on Mars, Ransom had noticed that young *séroni* acted as shepherds, and he thought of the Cyclops of Homer. On Perelandra he had many opportunities to observe the links between earthly mythology and cosmic reality. At the outset of his adventures he encounters "a small dragon covered with scales of red gold" [4] at the base of "a strange heraldically coloured tree loaded with yellow fruits and silver leaves," and immediately knows he is in the garden of the Hesperides.

Subsequently he sees mermen and mermaids swimming about, and recalls the terrestial myths of their existence. Most impressive of all his experiences, he talks with Mars and Venus face to face. (In *That Hideous Strength* we learn that each planetary *oyarsa* has a sort of representative or wraith on the earth, and that the ancient pagans had seen the doubles and made the disastrous mistake of worshipping them instead of Maleldil their creator.)

Very modern Jane Studdock, for all her graduate school primness, does not escape contact with mythology. Toward the end of *That Hideous Strength* she is busy preparing a room for the use of her maid and the maid's husband (who is due to be released from prison) when the house is invaded by a troupe of merry gnomelike little men wearing red caps and tassels. With them is a goddess of the marriage bed who bears a torch which makes flowers grow from whatever the flame touches. When Jane consults Ransom

[4] *Perelandra*, p. 41.

he explains that the particular area in which they are living seems to have strong bonds with the archaic past and that the presence of the resuscitated Merlin perhaps has something to do with the strange visitors.

No discussion of Lewis and mythology would be complete without mention of good and evil spirits. Almost every mythology in the world includes a belief in their existence; religions have frequently taught the necessity of soliciting the aid of good spirits (or alternatively, of propitiating the bad ones). Lewis, in his more matter-of-fact books, makes it clear that he believes in the existence of the Devil and his sub-devils, and also in angels. The devils are apparently the same as the "bent *eldil*" and *macrobes* of the novels, but the angels of the earth cannot be exactly equated with the ordinary *eldila* of other planets.

The situation on Thulcandra is unique. Alone among the planets, we are enemy-occupied territory: the bent *eldil* is prince of this world. On Malacandra it is possible for the *eldila* to go about their own business and only occasionally pause to offer their assistance to the *hnau*. On the earth, the constant machinations of the bent *eldil* and his subalterns have obliged the good *eldila* of our planet to constitute themselves into a sort of spiritual underground and bodyguard for besieged humankind. Dr. Dimble, in *That Hideous Strength,* advances the theory that everything in the universe is coming to a point; evil and good constantly growing more distinct. In St. Paul's time, he says, angels were not quite the same as they are today. Presumably, from struggling with the *macrobes* for nineteen hundred years they have become specialized in good deeds.

I think I should repeat my warning for the benefit of

anyone tempted to take all this too literally. Lewis, in his more imaginative books, does not profess to describe the specific realities of the universe: he is merely creating a myth of the *sort* of things that might plausibly exist. He *does* believe in the existence of devils and angels, and in the significance of mythology, but he is not set on proving that *eldila* roam the surface of Mars or soar in Deep Heaven.

There remains one question. Must myth, fact, and truth always remain separated? Lewis says they need not.[5] When God's purposes are fully achieved—when the "New Nature" has replaced the present Nature— "Every state of affairs in the New Nature will be the perfect expression of a spiritual state and every spiritual state the perfect informing of, and bloom upon, a state of affairs; one with it as the perfume with a flower or the 'spirit' of great poetry with its form."

He grants that fact and myth, the literal and the metaphorical, have had to be more and more sharply separated as intellectual analysis became more accurate, but the final goal is reunion: "Those who attain the glorious resurrection will see the dry bones clothed again with flesh, the fact and the myth remarried, the literal and the metaphorical rushing together."

In more ways than one, Lewis believes, we live in an interim period. Our restless minds rightly analyze everything, and separate truth, fact, and myth into their proper compartments. But the wise man will not forget that the separation is not the last word. In the crudest myths there are flashes of ultimate truth. The day is coming when the razor-edge of analysis will no longer divide the different aspects of one all-inclusive reality.

[5] *Miracles*, p. 192.

12. Last Things, First Things [*]

> *"And that," said Ransom, "will be the end?"*
> *Tor the King stared at him.*
> *"The end?" he said. "Who spoke of an end?"*
> *"The end of your world, I mean," said Ransom.*
> *"Splendor of Heaven!" said Tor. "Your thoughts are unlike ours. About that time we shall not be far from the beginning of all things. But there will be one matter to settle before the beginning rightly begins."*
> *"What is that?" asked Ransom.*
> *"Your own world," said Tor, "Thulcandra. The siege of your world shall be raised, the black spot cleared away, before the real beginning. . . ."*
>
> —*Perelandra,* pp. 226–227.

To hear a sermon on the Resurrection of the Body, the Final Judgment, or the non-atomic End of the World requires patience. The wise investigator will concentrate on the gospel halls in the humbler parts of the city. In time, if he visits enough of them, he will hear a preacher proclaim the Second Coming of Christ, and the sorting out of the sheep from the goats.

[*] This chapter was originally published in *Theology Today,* April 1949.

Only on rare and picturesque occasions do the newspapers mention eschatology—which once ranked with Christology and ecclesiology as one of the seven main branches of theology. And when they run a headline the word "eschatology" is not employed. They report that the Reverend So-and-So of some obscure sect has reread the Book of Revelation or studied the mathematics of the Pyramids to discover that the end of the world will come at midnight of a specified day. After the appointed day a brief human-interest story describes the disappointment of the faithful few as they knelt in their white sheets waiting for the end that refused to come. Meanwhile, the solid and reasonably permanent world continues with its daily business.

It is not that orthodox theology—Protestant or Catholic—has abandoned eschatology. It has embalmed it. The Apostles' Creed says that "Jesus Christ . . . shall come again, with glory, to judge both the quick and the dead," and adds, "I look for the Resurrection of the dead: And the Life of the world to come. Amen." But the "Amen" conveniently embraces a few million years during which the believer casually assumes that the catastrophic end of history is unlikely. In the same way, a scientist who knows all about the Second Law of Thermodynamics does not tremble with fear of freezing to death tomorrow.

Modernist Christianity has gone a step farther. It gets rid altogether of the Second Coming and its attendant events. The Kingdom of God becomes gradual Progress: an inching along toward a social millennium. Or else it is a purely "spiritual thing," and already exists in the hearts of the faithful.

More than forty years ago Albert Schweitzer, in *The*

Quest of the Historical Jesus, proved that whatever else Jesus may have been He was not a nineteenth-century liberal. He had never heard of inevitable progress. His thinking and teachings were in the framework of first-century Jewish eschatology—the science of "last things." Schweitzer went so far as to argue that Christ expected the end of the familiar world and its transformation into a supernatural new world within his own lifetime.

In his later book, *The Mysticism of Paul the Apostle,* Schweitzer portrays Paul not as the man who perversely complicated and spoiled the simple gospel of Jesus, but as a disciple who developed his Master's teachings with logic and consistency. To Paul, the supernatural transformation of the world had already begun. It began with the Resurrection of Christ. Step by step, the process will be completed.

So much for the four viewpoints: orthodox theology, which pushes the event off into a comfortably remote future; the gospel hall, prone to set a deadline; Modernist Christianity, explaining away or reinterpreting the "hard sayings" of Christ and Paul; and Schweitzer's theory, which is simply that Christ accepted the "world-view" of his time and mistakenly looked for the end of the world.

If Lewis must be classified, he belongs—as always—with the orthodox. But what for them is a remote eventuality becomes in his books a poetically vivid certainty. He sees the culminating event as powerfully as any tabernacle evangelist, but he attempts no timetables.

In *The Case for Christianity* he puts eschatology in a position of climax—the last paragraph of the book. He pictures God as planning an "invasion" of the earth, but meanwhile holding off to give people time to choose sides. When God invades—[1]

> . . . it's the end of the world. When the author walks on to the stage the play's over. God's going to invade, all right: but what's the good of saying you're on His side *then,* when you see the whole natural universe melting away like a dream and something else—something it never entered your head to conceive—comes crashing in; something so beautiful to some of us and so terrible to others that none of us will have any choice left.

Here there is a hint that the literal meaning of eschatology—"last things"—tells only half the story, and the less important half. Freed from the bonds of plain exposition, Lewis turns his imagination loose in the trilogy. The second of the novels, *Perelandra,* reports Ransom's conversation with Tor, the Adam of Venus, as Ransom prepares for his return journey to the earth. Far from being the end, God's intervention will be the real beginning of human history, Tor explains. Already the supernatural invasion is being planned. The inhabitants of the uncorrupted planets—both *hnau* and *eldila*—together with many men who once lived on the earth, will join forces with Maleldil Himself in the assault against the evil powers that hold "the Silent Planet" in servitude. As Maleldil and his host draw near the earth, the evil things will show themselves in all nakedness; plagues and horrors will cover the land and sea. But in the end Maleldil will conquer, and the earth will be received back into the comity of uncorrupted planets and its true name will be heard again.

[1] P. 56.

Ransom, still bewildered, says,[2] "What you call the beginning we are accustomed to call the Last Things."

"I do not call it the beginning," Tor answers. "It is but the wiping out of a false start in order that the world may *then* begin."

Thus forewarned, the reader of the third novel, *That Hideous Strength,* braces himself for the end—and beginning—of the world. Chapter by chapter he sees good and evil becoming more distinct as though two chemicals in a compound were being separated.

One reads on, expecting Christ to appear on clouds of glory and the dead to rise from their graves. But the expectation is disappointed. Lewis, daring as he is in depicting the undepictable, draws back. And Ransom, before leaving for Perelandra to dwell with Elijah and King Arthur, warns his disciples that the forces of evil have suffered one defeat but will strike back again before the end.

The eschatological note in Lewis's books has been growing more urgent. I believe it is totally absent in *The Pilgrim's Regress.* It becomes steadily more important as the three novels go along. One of his latest books—*Miracles*—stresses it most of all.

Many of the miracles of the New Testament are here presented as foreshadowings and samples of things to come. When Christ raised Lazarus from the dead He did something that Nature never does: He restored the past by reversing time. But this miracle was a modest one. Lazarus came back to life, but was the same Lazarus. A more striking example of what Lewis calls the "miracles of the New Creation" is afforded by Christ's walking on the water. At first it looks as though the thing were going to spread:

[2] P. 227.

St. Peter steps out on the waves and takes a few steps. But his faith fails him and he sinks. For a brief moment, a new relationship between spirit and matter has existed—matter the obedient servant of spirit—but the time is not ready for it. The episode is merely a foretaste of what will be a commonplace in the ultimate future.

The most striking miracles of the New Creation are the Transfiguration, the Resurrection, and the Ascension. In language curiously like that of Schweitzer, Lewis says of the Resurrection: [3]

> The New Testament writers speak as if Christ's achievement in rising from the dead was the first event of its kind in the whole history of the universe. He is the 'first fruits', the 'pioneer of life'. He has forced open a door that has been locked since the death of the first man. He has met, fought, and beaten the King of Death. Everything is different because He has done so. This is the beginning of the New Creation: a new chapter in cosmic history has opened.

In paragraph after paragraph Lewis attacks the "spiritualizers" who regard Christ's Resurrection as evidence for a purely spiritual, bodiless immortality in a mystical Heaven. Abruptly recalling one strange passage in the New Testament, he asks,[4] "If the truth is that after death there comes a negatively spiritual life, an eternity of mystical experience, what more misleading way of communicating it could possibly be found than the appearance of a human form which eats boiled fish?"

The body of the risen Christ can be touched and seen, but in some indescribable way it is different. On three

[3] P. 173.
[4] P. 176.

occasions the disciples do not immediately recognize their Master. What has happened to Christ defies the usual categories of thought. He has died, and come back to life; His new life is not purely "spiritual," nor is it completely a part of the old order of Nature. It is more as though He were already living in a New Nature, which partly interlocks with the old.

Lewis points out that we are prepared to believe in a reality with one floor (Nature) or in a reality with two floors (Nature and the Supernatural). But our habits of thought rebel against a picture of reality that would make it a skyscraper, with many floors between Nature, as we know it, and the unconditioned Absolute of God. And what the appearance of the risen Christ suggests is the existence of at least one intermediate floor.

When the New Nature comes into complete existence it will have points in common with the Old Nature, but will be different in at least one particular: the schism of matter and spirit (revealed today, according to Lewis, by our delight in dirty jokes and our fear of corpses) will be healed. Matter will obey spirit and be the better for it.

The Problem of Pain contains a "myth" (in the Socratic sense of what *may have been* historical fact) about the earliest men before the Fall. Lewis pictures them as having control over their organic processes. They could decide when they wanted to be hungry; perhaps even when they wanted to die. Having complete control over themselves, they held command over the animals. There was no schism of nature and spirit, no schism between man and beast.

Christ, to Lewis—as to orthodox Christianity—is the "new Adam," through whom humanity is to be restored to its original harmony with God. The final restoration will mean that man will once again have the same command over nature that Lewis attributes to the first men.

From all this it appears that Lewis's eschatology is not a simple affair. It involves "the end of the world," but that end is the real beginning. It will bring about a transformed Nature, heal schisms, and mark the culmination of the constantly increasing distinctness of good and evil.

Of all the great Christian teachers, perhaps St. Paul would feel most at home on reading Lewis's books. And like St. Paul, Lewis in *Miracles* hastens to warn his readers that theorizing about eventual glories must not turn their thoughts from the everyday virtues. "I most fully allow that it is of more importance for you or me to-day to refrain from one sneer or to extend one charitable thought to an enemy than to know all that angels and archangels know about the mysteries of the New Creation." [5]

There he might have left it, but Lewis—almost as much as G. K. Chesterton—dwells on the paradoxes of Christianity. "I will not admit," he says,[6] "that the things we have been discussing in the last few pages are of no importance for the practice of the Christian life. For I suspect that our conception of Heaven as *merely* a state of mind is not unconnected with the fact that the specifically Christian virtue of Hope has in our time grown so languid. Where our fathers, peering into the future, saw gleams of gold, we see only the mist, white, featureless, cold and never moving."

What sets Lewis apart as a non-conformist, even among most Christians, is the vividness of the gold in his religious imagination. And he has the ability to put it on paper.

[5] P. 193.
[6] P. 194.

13. Reason and Intellectual Climate *

> *Your man has been accustomed, ever since he was a boy, to have a dozen incompatible philosophies dancing about together inside his head. He doesn't think of doctrines as primarily "true" or "false," but as "academic" or "practical," "outworn" or "contemporary," "conventional" or "ruthless." Jargon, not argument, is your best ally in keeping him from the Church.*
>
> —*The Screwtape Letters*, p. 11.

The sales of *The Screwtape Letters* surprised everyone, author and publishers included. With the benefit of hindsight I should like to suggest that one reason for the popularity of the book is that it is an extremely neat example of turning the tables. Christians, long on the defensive and constantly accused of obscurantism, rejoiced to see Lewis—writing from the viewpoint of Hell—put the shoe on the other foot; he charged the secularists with intellectual fuzziness. And the secularists—those that had a sense of humor—read the book for a good-natured laugh at its sheer audacity.

In the course of thirty-one letters, His Infernal Excellency finds numerous occasions to warn Wormwood that Reason and Thought are menaces to the purposes of Hell.

* This chapter was originally published in the *Christian Century*, January 19, 1949.

"The trouble about argument is that it moves the whole struggle onto the Enemy's own ground. . . . By the very act of arguing, you awake the patient's reason; and once it is awake, who can foresee the result?" [1] Wormwood's job is not to reason with the patient but to befuddle him.

In another place Screwtape mentions that Hell has made Wormwood's task easier by encouraging the Evolutionary or Historical character of modern European thought. Instead of asking, about a proposed course of action, "Is it righteous? is it prudent? is it possible?" people are stimulated to wonder whether it fits in with the wave of the future. Thus they make their decisions in accordance with an imaginary time to come, which in its turn will be largely shaped by the choices they make. This, says Screwtape, gives the invisible agents of Hell an excellent opportunity to whisper suggestions to them while their minds are rattling around in the intellectual vacuum.

Later on Screwtape mentions the Historical point of view once more. Hell has conditioned the intellectual climate of Western Europe so that no one except the specialist reads old books—and then only to study influences and confute rival scholars. In this way, the present period of history is cut off from other periods, and there is little danger that the characteristic truths of the past will correct the typical errors of the present. ". . . thanks be to our Father and the Historical Point of View, great scholars are now as little nourished by the past as the most ignorant mechanic who holds that 'history is bunk'." [2]

Lewis's insistence that Reason must be used to arrive at truth comes out strongly in his attitude toward Chris-

[1] P. 12.
[2] P. 140.

tianity. He never urges its acceptance because it is "emotionally satisfying" or "socially useful." Screwtape quotes with approval a passage from a Christian writer who recommends his variety of Christianity on the ground that "only such a faith can outlast the death of old cultures and the birth of new civilizations," and comments, "You see the little rift? 'Believe this, not because it is true, but for some other reason.' That's the game." [3] (Screwtape, scornful of the niceties of scholarship, neglected to footnote the quotation. It was taken from Reinhold Niebuhr, *An Interpretation of Christian Ethics,* Harper & Brothers, New York and London, 1935, p. 34.)

As we have seen, *The Case for Christianity* is based entirely on the appeal to Reason, and in *Christian Behaviour* Lewis hammers home the point that faith is not unquestioning acceptance of the unproved. Rather, it is perseverance in belief after the belief has been thoroughly scrutinized and intellectually accepted. "I am not asking anyone to accept Christianity if his best reasoning tells him that the weight of the evidence is against it." [4] Faith enters the picture when belief is assailed by a *mood*—you are with scoffing friends or a situation arises in which it would be very convenient to break loose from the demands of Christian morality.

Lewis also has much to say about faith in the higher sense of complete trust in God, but nowhere does he equate it with the acceptance of beliefs contradictory to Reason.

This reliance upon Reason sets Lewis apart from a great many schools of Christian thought. Orthodox Protestantism has frequently disparaged Reason and contrasted it

[3] P. 120.
[4] P. 61.

with faith. The Neo-Orthodox movement in contemporary European Protestantism tends to set Reason and Revelation in opposition and view man as a creature who tremblingly accepts a salvation that his Reason cannot encompass. Modernist Christianity, though theoretically committed to Reason, often becomes so subjective that it dwells on the religious twinges of the individual and bypasses the question of whether Reason can work its way to any objective religious truth.

The insistence on Reason as the key to every kind of truth is found as early as *The Pilgrim's Regress.* In one part of the allegory, John of Puritania is shown imprisoned in a dungeon. A stone giant peers down through the iron grill, and his gaze makes anyone's body transparent. John sees people's lungs "panting like sponges," and the cancer inside an old man is horribly visible. The jailor brings food to the prisoners; if it is meat, he reminds them that they are eating corpses; if it is milk, he cracks a few jokes about the other secretions of the domestic cow.

John, who has not entirely lost his common sense, protests,[5] "You are trying to pretend that unlike things are like. You are trying to make us think that milk is the same sort of thing as sweat or dung."

The jailor smashes him in the teeth and turns to the others. "You see he is trying to argue. Now tell me, someone, what is argument?"

Master Parrot dutifully replies, "Argument is the attempted rationalization of the arguer's desires."

John is rescued by Reason—"a Titaness, a sun-bright virgin clad in complete steel, with a sword naked in her

[5] *The Pilgrim's Regress,* Sheed and Ward, Inc., New York, 1944, pp. 68–69. By permission of the publishers.

hand." [6] She slays the mountain-giant and releases any of the prisoners willing to emerge from the dungeon.

During his subsequent journeying with Reason, John learns that modern thought is shot through and through with intellectual dishonesty. The debunking to which he had been subjected in the dungeon was based on the unproved assumption that when a fair thing and a foul one resemble each other, the fair one must be a copy of the foul. The constant talk about "wish fulfillment" turns out to be an argument for God rather than against Him—the skeptics disbelieve in God because belief in Him would fill their lives with terror. And the reason for the muddle of contemporary thought? The secular thinkers have ceased to listen to the only people who know anything about ultimate truth. "They are younger sisters of mine," says Reason, "and their names are Philosophy and Theology." [7]

If *The Pilgrim's Regress* is a prolonged attack on secular pretensions to Reason, *The Great Divorce* contains Lewis's sharpest criticism of the mental haziness of Modernist Christianity. We have had occasion to discuss the apostate bishop several times already, and must glance at him again. When one of the saved breaks the news that the bishop has been in Hell for apostasy, the latter remonstrates: [8] "This is worse than I expected. Do you really think people are penalized for their honest opinions? Even assuming, for the sake of argument, that those opinions were mistaken?"

His friend tries—with no success whatever—to explain that the bishop's opinions had not been arrived at honestly;

[6] *Ibid.*, p. 71. By permission of the publishers.
[7] *Ibid.*, p. 77. By permission of the publishers.
[8] P. 32.

he had drifted along on a fashionable current of ideas, and plunged into it because it seemed modern and successful—and as a reward had become a bishop and a popular author. At no time had he honestly faced the fundamental question—whether after all the Supernatural might not in fact occur?

Miracles is as much a defense of Reason as of miracles. In one of the later chapters Lewis also tackles the question of moral judgments. Are they made with the Reason or with a different power? He holds to the first theory. "I believe that the primary moral principles on which all others depend are rationally perceived. We 'just see' that there is no reason why my neighbour's happiness should be sacrificed to my own, as we 'just see' that things which are equal to the same thing are equal to one another." [9]

The same argument is elaborated in *The Abolition of Man,* and the consequences of abandoning faith in Reason-and-morality are vividly dramatized in *That Hideous Strength.* Two of the characters—Frost and Wither—have repudiated the *Tao* so successfully that it is scarcely accurate to call them men: they are bundles of reflexes, and what they principally respond to is the promptings of demonic spirits. Other members of the N. I. C. E. are in process of being similarly dehumanized, and the goal sought is a world in which rational and moral man has been completely eliminated.

Lewis's constant defense of Reason sets him in opposition to many more groups than the behaviorists, "naturalists," and anti-rational schools of Christianity. On the political level he collides head-on with all who advocate thinking with the blood, whether racial or otherwise. In

[9] Pp. 43–44.

the realm of private morals he clashes with the glorifiers of "follow your impulses."

At no point in his thinking is Lewis more out of sympathy with the intellectual climate of the times than in his sturdy reliance upon Reason. Like a few other lone wolf thinkers he has observed the wholesale belittling of Reason which is almost the hall mark of the first half of the twentieth century. Certainly he has seen more clearly than most the intimate relation between Reason and morality, and the results if the two go down together. By his clear defense of Reason he is doing his best to make it intellectually respectable to think. And in so doing, he astonishes his readers with new ideas—straight from the darkness of the Middle Ages.

14. "Romanticism" *

You may have noticed that the books you really love are bound together by a secret thread. . . . Again, you have stood before some landscape, which seems to embody what you have been looking for all your life; and then turned to the friend at your side who appears to be seeing what you saw—but at the first words a gulf yawns between you, and you realise that this landscape means something totally different to him. . . . Are not all lifelong friendships born at the moment when at last you meet another human being who has some inkling (but faint and uncertain even in the best) of that something which you were born desiring, and which, beneath the flux of other desires and in all the momentary silences between the louder passions, night and day, year by year, from childhood to old age, you are looking for, watching for, listening for?

—*The Problem of Pain*, pp. 133–134.

The Pilgrim's Regress was an allegorical apology for "Romanticism" as well as for Christianity and Reason. The obscurity of the book was largely the by-product of the private meaning that the author unintentionally gave to the much-used word, Romanticism. In the third edition Lewis explains in clear prose what he meant by it.

* This chapter was originally published in *Advance,* March, 1949.

Romanticism, as he uses the word, is an experience of intense longing, which differs from other desires in two ways: the yearning is in itself a sort of delight, and a peculiar mystery envelops the object of desire. The latter may seem to be a distant hill, or a moment in the remote past; "perilous seas and faerie lands forlorn" or the perfect beloved. Whatever it is, it shifts ground the moment the supposed goal is reached. A child walks to the distant hill and discovers that a still farther hill is now the one fraught with "romance"; a man marries the perfect beloved and lives happily with her, but the strange yearning transfers to something else and continues to evade him.

Lewis contends that the experience is an extremely common one, and urges its importance: [1]

> It appeared to me therefore that if a man diligently followed this desire, pursuing the false objects until their falsity appeared and then resolutely abandoning them, he must come out at last into the clear knowledge that the human soul was made to enjoy some object that is never fully given —nay, cannot even be imagined as given—in our present mode of subjective and spatio-temporal experience. . . . This lived dialectic, and the merely argued dialectic of my philosophical progress, seemed to have converged on one goal; accordingly I tried to put them both into my allegory which thus became a defence of Romanticism (in my peculiar sense) as well as of Reason and Christianity.

John, at the beginning of the story, has an experience which turns his whole life into a quest. He is walking along the road when he hears sweet thin music coming from an

[1] *The Pilgrim's Regress,* Geoffrey Bles, Ltd., London, third edition, 1943, p. 10. By permission of the publishers.

unseen source behind him. A voice says, "Come." Beside the road he notices a stone wall with a glassless window in it. Peering through the opening, he sees a green wood full of primroses; a mist at the far end seems to part for a moment, revealing a calm sea and an island.

An overpowering sensation of sweetness seizes him, and the yearning for the island (often replaced by the desire to feel the yearning itself) stays with him after the vision fades. The rest of his life is a restless pilgrimage to find the island.

He tries everything. He lies with a "brown girl," but the illusion of fulfillment is brief. He journeys from philosopher to philosopher, tries their remedies, but none can help him. At last he accepts the advice of Mother Kirk. He comes up on the other side of *Peccatum Adae,* joins a vast throng of pilgrims, and sets forth on a long journey. Finally he sees his island in the distance, and the Guide explains that it is identical with the high mountains and the Landlord's castle which had loomed menacing on the horizon near his boyhood home. Once he had been near the island without knowing it. Now, after traveling almost the circumference of the world, he has reached the island from the other side. God, not brown girls, is the answer to the deepest desire of his heart.

The dominant symbols of the book are the "North" and the "South." The North stands for cold intellect, with its rigid systems and contempt for emotion. The South glorifies feeling at the expense of thought, and is fatally attracted by magic, pseudo-mysticism, etc. In the course of his wanderings John is threatened from both North and South and is saved only when he discovers the Main Road.

The idea of "Romanticism" (though the confusing word

is not used) appears again in the chapter on Heaven in *The Problem of Pain.* The treatment of the theological virtue of Hope in *Christian Behaviour* elaborates it further. The strange longing, Lewis says, is not for anything possible on earth. It is the thirst for Heaven. There are three ways that the desire can be dealt with: "The Fool's Way" is to trot from one inadequate goal to another—marry one woman and then divorce her for a second; spend a vacation at one scenic spot and next year try another—always vainly hoping to find *the* woman or *the* earthly paradise. "The Way of the Disillusioned 'Sensible Man' " is to dismiss the whole business as adolescent illusion, and make one's peace with the everyday world and its prosaic satisfactions. "The Christian way" is to reason that creatures are not born with desires impossible of fulfillment— [2]

> A duckling wants to swim: well, there is such a thing as water. Men feel sexual desire: well, there is such a thing as sex. If I find in myself a desire which no experience in this world can satisfy, the most probable explanation is that I was made for another world. . . . I must take care, on the one hand, never to despise, or be unthankful for, these earthly blessings and on the other, never to mistake them for the something else of which they are only a kind of copy, or echo, or mirage.

It seems to me that insufficient attention has been paid to Lewis's theory of "Romanticism." He does not lean upon it as heavily as he does upon Reason, but it offers a complementary road to religious commitment. When two roads lead to the same city you suspect that the city is worth reaching.

[2] Pp. 57–58.

But there is more to it than this, and here I speak personally. The concept of "Romanticism" makes it possible for the individual better to understand a strange variety of experiences which seem at first glance so subjective that they cannot be communicated to others. "Romanticism" is a clue to their meaning, and the key to unlocking the hidden meaning of much that is otherwise bewildering and almost meaningless in poetry and the arts. Literary criticism could profit from a realization of this: for example, I can think of many passages in Wordsworth's poetry that suddenly become fraught with meaning in the light of Lewis's explanation.

The process of "growing up" is often misunderstood. It does not consist of ridiculing and forsaking what was most deeply significant in childhood. Rather, it means *understanding* the truths that were once perceived in flashes, and fitting the fragments of truth together. A phrase of music, the sight of birds flying high overhead, the lonely tulip poplar standing golden on a distant autumn hill—these are the clues to mysteries that the proud adult neglects at the risk of drying up into something less than fully human.

15. The Christian Day by Day *

> *God may be more than moral goodness: He is not less. The road to the promised land runs past Sinai.*
>
> —*The Problem of Pain,* p. 53.
>
> *Every Christian is to become a little Christ. The whole purpose of becoming a Christian is simply that: nothing else.*
>
> —*Beyond Personality,* p. 24.

The blueprints of Christian morality that Lewis offers are sternly orthodox but curiously alluring. He has the great advantage of not being a puritan. When John the pilgrim left Puritania he left it for good.

To take a trivial example, Lewis shows himself irritated at the common habit of restricting the word "temperance" to teetotalism.[1] "Temperance referred not specially to drink, but to all pleasures; and it meant not abstaining, but going the right length and no further. It is a mistake to think that Christians ought all to be teetotallers; Mohammedanism, not Christianity, is the teetotal religion." (The *hrossa,* we learn in *Out of the Silent Planet,* have an alcoholic beverage and sometimes grow slightly high on their gayer nights.)

God's approval of sensible pleasures runs through Lewis's

* This chapter was originally published in the *Catholic World,* February, 1949.

[1] *Christian Behaviour,* p. 9.

thinking about morality, but this is not always obvious at a first reading. His treatment of sex would not strike the lovers of modern fiction as a glorification of pleasure. Yet, as Lewis proceeds to talk about it, the ancient ideal of monogamy becomes strangely enticing. The sexual act, as he explains it, is not a casual intimacy but the means whereby two individuals become literally a single organism—"one flesh." Marriage is the way the union is made a complete, all-around one—a growing together that is spiritual, intellectual, and psychological, as well as physical. The glamor of "falling in love" may be brief-lived, but something deeper and steadier takes its place.

Still more astonishing is Lewis's success in sweetening the bitter news that wives should obey their husbands. The argument in *Christian Behaviour* is pragmatic. Since marriage is meant to be permanent, there has to be some way of resolving a stalemate. It is best for the man to cast the deciding vote because by nature he is less belligerent toward the outer world: [2]

> A woman is primarily fighting for her own children and husband against the rest of the world. . . . The function of the husband is to see that this natural preference of hers isn't given its head. He has the last word in order to protect other people from the intense family patriotism of the wife. If anyone doubts this, let me ask a simple question. If your dog has bitten the child next door, or your child has hurt the dog next door, which would you sooner have to deal with, the master of that house or the mistress?

More deftly he continues the argument for wifely obedience in *That Hideous Strength*. Jane has grown up resenting

[2] Pp. 36–37.

the crude male tendency to admire her looks rather than her brains and inner self. This makes her impatient with Mark and his clumsy male impetuosity. Her tottering marriage is saved by Ransom, who convinces her that male aggressiveness is only a part of a cosmic thing: the "masculine." In the presence of God (the complete "masculine") men and women alike are "feminine." This doctrine is not initially pleasing to Jane, but in time a seductive fragrance seems to accompany it; Ransom also succeeds in persuading her that obedience is an "erotic necessity." As the book draws to an end, and Mark returns, she is ready to obey him.

I see that I have followed the path of least resistance by dwelling at length on sex. In common parlance (even in some sermons) the word morality means sexual morality. But Lewis himself is quick to point out that sexual sins are not the worst. They come from the animal self, whereas the blackest sins of all are not animal but spiritual: [8] ". . . a cold, self-righteous prig who goes regularly to Church may be far nearer to hell than a prostitute. But, of course, it is better to be neither."

At times, Lewis hints at a stage where morality, having been perfectly fulfilled, is transcended by something greater—but that is the end of a very long road, whose terminus is Heaven, and the road itself is marked by the familiar milestones of the ancient commandments. The Christian's object, as Lewis sees it, is not simply to obey the commandments in specific situations but to acquire the set of character that will make them part of his nature. His decisions, minute by minute, are crucial because they affect the central core of his being. Each choice brings him

[8] *Christian Behaviour*, p. 29.

a little nearer to God or pushes him a little farther into the nothingness.

Lewis does not pretend that the process is an easy one. It involves nothing less than a complete surrender to the will of God—as though a lump of clay turned itself over to the sculptor and said, "Do with me as you will." It means killing a swarm of imperious desires, most of all the root of nearly every other evil: stubborn, self-seeking, jealous Pride.

We are given no hope that mere time can perform miracles. Lewis does not equate evolving with improvement: [4]

> We are not living in a world where all roads are radii of a circle and where all, if followed long enough, will therefore draw gradually near and finally meet at the centre: rather in a world where every road, after a few miles, forks into two, and each of those into two again, and at each fork you must make a decision.

The day-by-day decisions mount up to the final Yes or No. If the answer is Yes, the Christian's destiny is to become a "little Christ," able to bear the searing light of God's presence and endure the happiness of Heaven.

Lewis touches on two points famous in theological controversy. Despite his insistence that every one of us is deeply scarred and twisted by the Fall of man, he denies the doctrine of Total Depravity. "I disbelieve that doctrine, partly on the logical ground that if our depravity were total we should not know ourselves to be depraved, and partly because experience shows us much goodness in human nature." [5]

[4] *The Great Divorce,* pp. v–vi.
[5] *The Problem of Pain,* pp. 54–55.

About Faith versus Works his position is less simple. He believes that both are needed. A serious moral effort will show you that you can't be perfect through your own endeavors; when you come to recognize this, only faith in Christ will save you from despair; out of that faith will inevitably come good works. For his text he takes the biblical injunction which combines the two ideas: [6] "Work out your own salvation with fear and trembling, for it is God which worketh in you . . ."

Many friendly critics have been troubled because Lewis says little about the application of Christianity to economics, politics, and the like. The omission would not have been so striking in the pietistic seventeenth century, but today, what with the "social gospel" and many attempts to evolve a Christian sociology from orthodoxy, the things passed over in silence are striking. A Christian, guided by Lewis, knows how to meet the machinations of Screwtape in almost every situation involving three or four people, but he is left without guidance when he goes to the polls or participates in a panel discussion on foreign policy.

It is true that Lewis expresses a definite opinion about one dilemma which torments many modern Christians as they come up against the demands of society. He is strongly against pacifism. His arguments, developed in *Christian Behaviour* and *The Screwtape Letters,* are convincing enough to the non-pacifist, though I suspect they would strike a pacifist as being unduly legalistic.

With this one exception, the generalization holds. I asked Lewis why he said so little about social Christianity, and he simply answered, "That's not my vocation." He hastened to add that he did not believe every writer on Christianity

[6] Philippians 2:12–13, quoted in *Christian Behaviour,* pp. 69–70.

should avoid the subject: he merely felt that he was not the one to handle it.

I rather suspect that part of his reluctance comes from an extreme fear of getting involved in "Christianity and—" —the convenient tag invented by Screwtape to describe a viewpoint which values Christianity because it can be used as the *means* toward something else. It was also clear from Lewis's remarks that he is pessimistic about the immediate prospects of bringing Christianity to bear on the more violent problems of society. "The main political problem of the Christian today is how to survive as a Christian in a non-Christian society," he said. The ominous shadow of the N. I. C. E. looms dark in Lewis's mind. He believes that an era of religious persecution may be nearer than anyone expects. In the English-speaking countries he does not think it will involve beasts in the arena: rather, Christians will be turned over to psychiatrists and subjected to treatment "for their own good."

Where he touches on the social implications of Christianity in his books, Lewis emphasizes that detailed plans must come from Christian specialists. "'The application of Christian principles, say, to Trades Unionism or education, must come from Christian Trades Unionists and Christian schoolmasters: just as Christian literature comes from Christian novelists and dramatists—not from the bench of Bishops getting together and trying to write plays and novels in their spare time," he says in *Christian Behaviour*.[7] Elsewhere, in discussing usury, he declines to say whether it is right or wrong: the problem is one for Christian economists to answer.

Lewis fights an occasional skirmish with the people who

[7] Pp. 14–15.

scoff about "pie in the sky." To him it is not the opiate of the people: [8]

> The Apostles themselves, who set on foot the conversion of the Roman Empire, the great men who built up the Middle Ages, the English Evangelicals who abolished the Slave Trade, all left their mark on Earth, precisely because their minds were occupied with Heaven. It is since Christians have largely ceased to think of the other world that they have become so ineffective in this. Aim at Heaven and you will get earth "thrown in": aim at earth and you will get neither.

In *The Problem of Pain* [9] he admits that Christianity forbids us to hope that any economic or political-system can ever create a complete heaven on earth, but he argues that this should not and does not have a depressing effect on work for social amelioration; a realization of mankind's common miseries is as good a spur as the romantic hopes of utopian perfection which can lead only to brutal methods and eventual despair.

For one tantalizing brief instant Lewis does vouchsafe a thumbnail sketch of what he conceives a Christian society to be.[10] Its economy would be rather left-wing. There would be no parasites living on the work of others, no producers of silly luxury items and writers of ads for useless goods. On the other hand, the society would be ceremonious, even aristocratic in its customs: men would obey the properly constituted magistrates (and greet them with outward marks of respect); children and wives would show

[8] P. 55.
[9] P. 102.
[10] *Christian Behaviour*, pp. 15–16.

similar reverence to parents and husbands. In the third place, the Christian society would be a cheerful one, full of rejoicing and song, and inclined to brand worry a sin.

One might wish that Lewis, even though he is not a social science expert, would elaborate this sketch in some future book. But he is doubtless right that no one would be entirely happy with his proposed society. As he points out in *Christian Behaviour,* the leftists would like its economy while deploring its manners; the conservatives would damn it as radicalism. "A Christian society," Lewis insists, "is not going to arrive until most of us really want it: and we are not going to want it until we become fully Christian. And so, as I warned you, we are driven inward—driven on from social matters to religious matters. For the longest way round is the shortest way home." [11]

Lewis is not an avid reader of the daily headlines, and his political pessimism forbids him to look for the immediate flowering forth of a Christian society. The passage I have just summarized is his brief hint of what such a society might be like, and I doubt that his social thinking goes much farther. Indeed, in talking with him I sometimes felt that his casual remarks on current problems suggested the conditioned reflexes of the upper middle class rather than the stimulating ideas he set down in *Christian Behaviour.* He is not a Niebuhr or a Maritain, and does not pretend to be one. His vocation, as he sees it, is to do spadework—win people to Christianity itself—and once they are won, those who are qualified to wield the draftsman's pencil can start work on the blueprints.

[11] P. 18.

16. Science and Satan

> *Nothing I can say will prevent some people from describing this lecture as an attack on science. I deny the charge, of course: and real Natural Philosophers (there are some now alive) will perceive that in defending value I defend* INTER ALIA *the value of knowledge, which must die like every other when its roots in the* TAO *are cut. But I can go further than that. I even suggest that from Science herself the cure might come.*
>
> —*The Abolition of Man,* p. 47.

One question frequently asked about C. S. Lewis is, "Does he think science is the child of Satan?" The villain of the first two novels is a physicist-turned-biologist, who obligingly lends his body as well as his soul to the Devil, so that the latter can incarnate himself and evade the divine sanitary regulations which forbid him to travel beyond the orbit of the moon. After Ransom, the heroic Christian philologist, slays Weston in the caverns of Perelandra, more villains are needed—and are promptly supplied in the third novel by a whole nestful of scientists hatching dire plots in the N. I. C. E.—"the first-fruits of that constructive fusion between the state and the laboratory on which so many thoughtful people base their hopes of a better world." [1] It does rather seem that science takes a

[1] *That Hideous Strength,* p. 13.

beating in several of his books. But the matter will stand closer examination.

One possible misconception can be quickly brushed aside. Lewis is not anti-scientific in a Fundamentalist sense. He is not troubled by the "conflict between science and religion" for the reason that his theology does not conflict with anything that science has so far discovered or is ever likely to discover. One cannot imagine him voting to prohibit the teaching of evolution in the schools of Britain.

Somehow the subject of the N. I. C. E. came up once when I was with Lewis and I asked him whether he was against science. He answered—with unusual warmth—that he was not. "Science is neither an enemy nor a friend," he said. "Science is not a *person!*"

When I pressed him for some comments on the N. I. C. E. he said that the point had been missed by many readers. The moral is not that science or scientists are launching an attack on humanity, but simply that anyone who is an enemy of humanity would claim the prestige of science. (In this connection, it is true that remarkably little scientific research seems to be carried on at the N. I. C. E. The routine activities are more those of a convention of witches.)

Lewis added he had noticed that the "pure sciences" seem to have no dehumanizing effect on those who study them, but that the closer a science approaches to human affairs the more it tends to strip its specialists of their humanity; sociologists and psychologists are in greater peril than chemists and mathematicians. This recalls the counsel of Screwtape: [2]

[2] *The Screwtape Letters,* p. 14.

> Above all, do not attempt to use science (I mean, the real sciences) as a defence against Christianity. They will positively encourage him to think about realities he can't touch and see. There have been sad cases among the modern physicists. If he must dabble in science, keep him on economics and sociology. . . .

Hengist, the gruff old chemist in *That Hideous Strength,* doubtless speaks as Lewis's mouthpiece when he says: [8] "There *are* no sciences like Sociology. . . . I happen to believe that you can't study men; you can only get to know them, which is quite a different thing. Because you study them, you want to make the lower orders govern the country and listen to classical music, which is balderdash. You also want to take away from them everything which makes life worth living and not only from them but from everyone except a parcel of prigs and professors."

Lewis's most carefully reasoned treatment of the sciences in general is contained in *The Abolition of Man.* There he analyzes the glib phrase, "man's conquest of nature," and concludes that the process really means some men's domination of other men by the use of nature. For example, contraceptives—a development of applied science—give one generation power over all succeeding generations by limiting the number of lives brought into being. It is a victory over nature in one sense, but still more the victory of living men over the men that might be.

Lewis's nightmare, as revealed in this book and fictionally pictured in *That Hideous Strength,* is that a handful of men will get control of the techniques of science—in-

[8] Pp. 72–73.

cluding applied psychology—and use their power to create a new "human nature" for everyone else. The very desire to do this would mean that the conditioners were already outside the framework of the *Tao*. Being on the outside they would have nothing to guide them except chance impulses, and the new human nature they might choose to instil in the masses would in all likelihood be a hideous one. If the conditioning were maintained effectively the alteration might also be permanent. (Compare Aldous Huxley's *Brave New World*!)

To Lewis the origin of modern science is disquietingly linked with the Renaissance dabbling in magic: [4]

> The fact that the scientist has succeeded where the magician failed has put such a wide contrast between them in popular thought that the real story of the birth of Science is misunderstood. . . . There was very little magic in the Middle Ages; the sixteenth and seventeenth centuries are the high noon of magic. The serious magical endeavour and the serious scientific endeavour are twins: one was sickly and died, the other strong and throve.

He grants that some of these early scientists were motivated by a pure love of knowledge, but contends that at the very least the modern scientific movement "was born in an unhealthy neighbourhood and at an inauspicious hour." [5] Both magic and applied science are mainly concerned with how to subdue reality to human wishes, whereas the older "wisdom" sought to subdue the soul to reality.

[4] *The Abolition of Man*, pp. 47–48.
[5] *Ibid.*, p. 49.

The suggestion that magic and science have a submerged kinship comes out in *The Screwtape Letters,* with a hopeful prophecy of the future: [6]

> I have great hopes that we shall learn in due time how to emotionalise and mythologise their science to such an extent that what is, in effect, a belief in us [demons], (though not under that name) will creep in while the human mind remains closed to belief in the Enemy. . . . If once we can produce our perfect work—the Materialist Magician, the man, not using, but veritably worshipping, what he vaguely calls "Forces" while denying the existence of "spirits"—then the end of the war will be in sight.

In *That Hideous Strength,* Screwtape has his wish. The lords of the N. I. C. E. are devil-worshipers—only they call the devils "macrobes." Instructed by their masters they endeavor to capture Merlin, so as to effect a junction between his ancient magic and the techniques of ultramodern science. By the combination of the two they hope to rule the world (for the benefit of the macrobes, of course.) When the plans end in disaster the macrobes demand their proper due. Two of the initiates guillotine one of the others, chanting as they do so: [7]

> "Ouroborindra!
> Ouroborindra!
> Ouroborindra ba-ba-hee!"

One of the survivors then stabs his companion to death, picks up the guillotined head and presents it to the artificially preserved Head through which the macrobes have been accustomed to speak.

[6] Pp. 39–40.
[7] Pp. 422–423.

All this sounds like melodrama, and is. For that reason too little attention has been paid to it. What Lewis in his fantastic way is trying to say is simply that science is good and wholesome only within the framework of the *Tao*—that once it is hailed as an end in itself and all other human values swept aside the door is opened for demons to swarm into the well-swept room and use the pretensions and techniques of science for their own purposes.

It is a viewpoint that cannot be waved aside. Since the invention and use of the atomic bomb, the ambiguity of science has begun to penetrate the popular consciousness; many atomic scientists have issued warnings not too different, except in choice of words, from Lewis's.

That Lewis is not a science-hater is evident from the passage I cited at the head of this chapter. He hopes to see the scientists themselves provide the cure for the perversions of science. As he tentatively sketches the new Natural Philosophy that he hopes to see develop, it would be one which would "explain" without "explaining away." It would study the parts but always remember that the sum of the parts does not explain the whole; it would be ever mindful that the systematized facts of science are an abstraction from ultimate reality, and a degree less real. "Its followers would not be free with the words *only* and *merely*. In a word, it would conquer Nature without being at the same time conquered by her and buy knowledge at a lower cost than that of life." [8]

[8] *The Abolition of Man,* p. 49.

17. Influences

A doctoral dissertation could be written on the writers who have influenced Lewis. The scope of his reading is remarkably catholic, and traces of almost everything he has read can be found somewhere in his books. His solid background in the Latin and Greek classics has been supplemented by almost the entire *corpus* of English literature, great familiarity with the medieval literature of western Europe, a thorough knowledge of ancient Norse mythology and a reasonable acquaintance with Celtic lore. Add to all this the Bible and modern American scientifiction and the result is a rich if heterogeneous mixture.

Of necessity I shall speak of only a few of the writers who have left the greatest imprint on Lewis—either by influencing his ideas or his literary technique. At the head of the list stands George Macdonald (1824–1905), the Scotch minister whose name was once a household word to children brought up on *The Princess and Curdie, The Prince and the Goblin,* and *At the Back of the North Wind.* Newer books expounding the usefulness of tractors or narrating the adventures of socially conscious chipmunks have largely deprived today's children of Macdonald's wonderland fantasies, and his adult books—*Unspoken Sermons* and fairyland novels like *Lilith* and *Phantastes*—are even more neglected.

Lewis has several times described his first encounter

with Macdonald, when, about the age of eighteen, he chanced to buy a copy of *Phantastes* and found himself plunged into a world of satisfying imagination fragrant with a peculiar goodness that later he was obliged to identify with Christianity. To analyze the power and depth of Macdonald I find no easy task. It does not lie in his style: Lewis can write circles around his master. There seems no way of avoiding the word holiness. It is a holiness at once gentle and inexorable: the insight of a man who sees in God's wrath the expression of His absolute love. To Macdonald, nothing less than everything is God's demand, and God's return is nothing less than everything.

But I do not intend a theological treatment of Macdonald. It is enough to say that his conviction that nothing of value on the earth is lost in Heaven, his emphasis on final and total surrender to God, and his Christocentric theology are all echoed and developed in Lewis. Macdonald baptized Lewis's imagination, as the latter puts it, and it seems evident that the example of Macdonald encouraged Lewis to use fanciful literary forms for expressing his Christianity.

Another influence of a profound but less obvious sort is that of Charles Williams. The two men had occasionally met before World War II, but their close friendship dates from the time when the Oxford University Press moved to Oxford to escape the blitz. Speaking of Williams' sudden death in 1945 Lewis writes with a personal intensity rare in his books: [1] "No event has so corroborated my faith in the next world as Williams did simply by dying. When the

[1] *Essays Presented to Charles Williams,* Oxford University Press, London, New York, Toronto, 1947, p. xlv. By permission of the publishers.

idea of death and the idea of Williams thus met in my mind, it was the idea of death that was changed."

Williams is almost unknown in America, though an American publishing house, Pellegrini and Cudahy, has recently begun bringing out his novels. In England he was avidly read and ardently admired by a small circle of Christian intellectuals, including T. S. Eliot and Dorothy Sayers. His literary output was as varied as Lewis's—poetry, critical essays, theological treatises, novels. His poetry, though extremely difficult, is much superior to Lewis's, but as a prose stylist he lacks the easy lucidity and wit of his friend.

Much of the influence that Williams had on Lewis was of the intangible sort that comes when two friends sit together over their mugs of cider and talk about anything that pops into their heads. Williams' novels, if I am not mistaken, had a more direct impact. The first of his "theological thrillers," *War in Heaven,* appeared in 1930, eight years before Lewis essayed the same genre with *Out of the Silent Planet.* Williams' subsequent novels, eagerly read by Lewis, served to confirm Lewis in his belief that the fantastic novel could be used for serious philosophic purposes.

As I mentioned in an earlier chapter, Lewis and Williams took turns reading their work-in-progress to each other; Williams was working on *All Hallows' Eve* at the same time that Lewis was writing *Perelandra.* I think I can see resemblances between *All Hallows' Eve* and the concluding novel of Lewis's trilogy, *That Hideous Strength.* The magician, Simon Leclerc, who has created two doubles of himself and planted them in strategic parts of the world to seduce the unthinking multitudes so that in time he may hold a world conference with himself and gain mastery of the globe immediately suggests the schemes of the N. I. C. E.

Less clear-cut similarities between the two men's novels also come to mind. The casual flitting back and forth between the every-day world and the spiritual world in Williams' novels may well have stimulated Lewis to break down the barriers separating the natural and the supernatural when he came to write his interplanetary romances.

What I have said is admittedly speculation. And it may be that the importance of Williams is not so much that he suggested specific plot material or literary techniques to Lewis as that the friendship with the older man deepened Lewis's imagination and religious insight, to the enrichment of whatever he subsequently wrote.

The literary ancestry of Lewis's novels involves a number of strands. The general type had been created by Jules Verne, H. G. Wells, and numerous authors of pulp fiction. These models, however, provided a framework for little more than startling adventures. To David Lindsay, author of the almost forgotten novel, *A Voyage to Arcturus* (1920), Lewis attributes the discovery that scientifiction can be used as a medium for recounting spiritual adventures.

The novel is written with what appears a gnostic hatred of the material world. The main character (one can hardly call him the hero), boasting the name of Maskull, journeys via spaceship with companions Nightspore and Krag to Tormance, a planet circling around the star Arcturus. He has a series of adventures, usually involving spiritual temptation and most often culminating in murder. At length the reader is vouchsafed a vision of God, in which the deity is seen as a vulgar, selfish being who creates life for the sensual pleasure it gives Him, and by his act inflicts untold misery on spirit thus imprisoned in flesh.

The theology of *A Voyage to Arcturus* is not to Lewis's taste, but he praises the book as a pioneer extension of the scope of interplanetary fiction: [2]

> The physical dangers, which are plentiful, here count for nothing: it is we ourselves and the author who walk through a world of spiritual dangers which makes them seem trivial. There is no recipe for writing of this kind. But part of the secret is that the author (like Kafka) is recording a lived dialectic. His Tormance is a region of the spirit. He is the first writer to discover what 'other planets' are really good for in fiction.

Other writers who have influenced Lewis in a more general way include such a grab-bag as Dr. Johnson, G. K. Chesterton, and the William Morris of the narrative poems and prose romances. Among the theologians (in addition to Macdonald) he has been especially attracted to St. Augustine, St. Athanasius (whose battle against the Arian heresy was strikingly similar to Lewis's war on Modernist Christianity), and Hooker (especially the earlier writings). He told me that he uses Thomas Aquinas as a convenient reference work but has not been greatly influenced by him in general, though he may have indirectly absorbed a good deal of Aquinas *via* Dante.

I doubt that one can label Lewis either an Aristotelian or a Platonist. His neat way of thought perhaps suggests Aristotle, but the role that "universals" play in his thinking brings him close to Plato. Perhaps more directly influential

[2] C. S. Lewis, "On Stories," in *op. cit.*, p. 98. By permission of the publishers.

than either of the philosophic giants is Boethius, whose sixth-century work, *The Consolation of Philosophy,* was the favorite reading of the Middle Ages. To it Lewis is directly indebted for his solution of what he calls the "pseudo-problem" of predestination and free will. Anyone curious to trace the influence of Boethius will find it toward the close of *The Great Divorce,* with the imagery of the chess game supplied by Sir Thomas Browne's *Religio Medici.*

This very cursory survey of influences makes it clear that Lewis does not elevate "originality" into a cult. In his critical writings he argues that not originality but the expression of something of universal profit is the thing desired from an author. He practices what he preaches. He takes ideas and literary techniques from any convenient source with the freedom of a Chaucer or Shakespeare, but —like his more distinguished fellow-writers—he thoroughly assimilates and transmutes. The paradoxical result is that Lewis's books give an impression of extreme originality. The mysterious chemistry of the mind has brought everything into harmony, and the strangely assorted ingredients add not confusion but richness and body.

18. The Psychologist

> *. . . do make quite sure that you are judging me by what you really know from your own experience and from watching the lives of your friends, and not by ideas you have derived from novels and films. This is not so easy to do as people think.*
>
> —*Christian Behaviour*, p. 32.

If C. S. Lewis were a successful business man, a physicist, a lawyer, or even a professor of psychology, the general reader would be willing to assume that he knew something about human nature. It is well known, however, that he is none of these. He is an Oxford don, living and lecturing in one of the most charming ivory towers left in this depressing world. To cap the climax, he is a bachelor.

For all these cogent reasons it is commonly taken for granted that he dwells in a never-never land, pleasantly dividing his time between Christian mythology and Chaucerian chronology, while the busy world and its complexes leave him untouched and unperceiving.

The temptation is strong to pause and argue the philosophic presuppositions in this line of reasoning. It is not necessarily true that the best war novels are written by men who have personally dug latrine ditches; it is certainly true that the best novel about the Oakies was written by a man who was not an Oakie. But more to the point, let us look at Lewis's books.

Presumably no writer is completely universal in his grasp of human nature. Chaucer could never have created Hamlet; if Shakespeare had tried to depict the Miller he would surely have made him into a low-comedy clown. Lewis, too, has his specialties, as well as extensive blank spots.

To begin with the specialties—he possesses an extraordinary understanding of religious psychology. It does not embrace every facet—for example, he shies away from mysticism except in a few cases (like Jane Studdock's encounter with God as she walks in the garden), and even in these, there is little hint of the wordless depths demanded by Christopher Isherwood and Gerald Heard.

Lewis deals with a more bread-and-butter kind of religious experience. At the very beginning of *The Screwtape Letters* he singles out the unconscious spiritual pride of the recent convert when he goes to church: [1] "Your patient, thanks to Our Father below, is a fool. Provided that any of those neighbours sing out of tune, or have boots that squeak, or double chins, or odd clothes, the patient will quite easily believe that their religion must therefore be somehow ridiculous."

A little later on Screwtape holds forth on the frequency of "dry periods" in the life of a Christian. These times, when God seems remote and prayer becomes unreal, are merely the result of the "law of Undulation." Man being half spirit and half animal, cannot keep an even psychological keel in religion, appetite, affection, or anything else.

That no man's land where religion and conduct meet provides Lewis with some of his best opportunities to show human nature in action. He seldom dramatizes; more

[1] P. 16.

often he selects the details that appear scarcely more significant than the quick movement that lights a cigarette, but sees into them with an insight that gives them an urgent meaningfulness.

The Screwtape Letters—his richest manual of psychology—is full of such instances. At first glance there seems nothing too fearful in the fondness the patient's mother has for tiny helpings of food and her insistence on "an egg properly boiled, or a slice of bread properly toasted." [2] But to the shrewd eyes of Screwtape she is guilty of a very desirable kind of gluttony—desirable because she will never call it by its true name and because it is a source of unlimited friction between her and everyone around her.

In the same way, the patient does not seem unduly sinful when he assumes, "My time is my own," and gets irritated at unexpected interruptions. But as Screwtape analyzes the innocent-sounding phrase it appears that the patient has been guilty of unmitigated presumption: none of his time is his own by right. He did not create time; furthermore, he is committed to total service of the Enemy, and should be grateful for any occasional half hour given him for his own amusement.

An example of a habit that hovers between harmless silliness and a definite vice is the quiet assumption on the part of the patient's fiancée that non-Christians are just too ridiculous and stupid for words. Screwtape regretfully concludes that little spiritual harm can come to the girl from this—it is mere ignorance and naïveté on a level with believing that the fish-knives used in neighboring families are "not real fish-knives" at all. But if the patient can be per-

[2] P. 87.

suaded to ape his fiancée's mannerism, he will overdo it and the possibilities of spiritual pride will be excellent.

The quiet irritations of the family circle are analyzed with uncomfortable exactness in one letter: [3]

> In civilized life domestic hatred usually expresses itself by saying things which would appear quite harmless on paper (the words are not offensive) but in such a voice, or at such a moment, that they are not far short of a blow in the face. To keep this game up you and Glubose [the old lady's tempter] must see to it that each of these two fools has a sort of double standard. . . . Hence from every quarrel they can both go away convinced, or very nearly convinced, that they are quite innocent. You know the kind of thing: "I simply ask her what time dinner will be and she flies into a temper."

Screwtape reaches his greatest depth of insight when he discourses on "unselfishness" (the word that the Philological Arm of Hell has substituted for the more positive virtue, charity). We are shown a group of people, each of whom vies with the others in the race to be unselfish. Each insists on doing what he assumes the others want to do: no one will admit to having any desires of his own. In the end they all settle on some activity that no one really likes; bad tempers and feelings of unappreciated martyrdom are delightfully aroused.

We have seen that in *Christian Behaviour* Lewis characterizes woman as more fiercely devoted to family loyalties than is the diplomatic male. Elsewhere he enumerates at least three other differences between the sexes.

Screwtape points out that men think of "unselfishness"

[3] Pp. 22–23.

as leaving people alone, while women take it to mean actively doing things for others (this is an excellent ground for quarrels). He also observes that fatigue makes women talk more and men less (another occasion for quarrels). But the keenest contribution made by Lewis to the psychology of the sexes is put in the mouth of MacPhee: [4]

> "The cardinal difficulty," said MacPhee, "in collaboration between the sexes is that women speak a language without nouns. If two men are doing a bit of work, one will say to the other, 'Put this bowl inside the bigger bowl which you'll find on the top shelf of the green cupboard.' The female for this is, 'Put that in the other one in there.' And then if you ask them, 'in where?' they say, 'in *there*, of course.' . . ."

The Great Divorce is a gallery of dreary men and women who have damned themselves into futility by vices that do not make startling reading. There is the pharasaical man, who has always done his duty and never run afoul of the law: [5] "If I wanted a drink I paid for it and if I took my wages I done my job, see?" He stands on the border of Heaven, demanding his rights, and will never understand that in his legalistic righteousness he was harsh to everyone with whom he worked and was hated by all during life.

A grumbling old woman, now scarcely more than a grumble; another woman who dominated and ruined her husband's life—the drab procession passes by.

Few writers have specialized in the psychology of the college teacher—his suppressed hopes, frustrations, secret uncertainties. Lewis, writing from the inside, is able to do

[4] *That Hideous Strength,* p. 190.
[5] P. 25.

this. Mark Studdock is the epitome of all nervous and ambitious young instructors. He worries about the wad of cotton-wool on his shaving cut when he goes to meet the great men of the N. I. C. E.; he is pitifully eager to be accepted by the "Progressive Element" or any other coterie; his whole day is brightened if a weighty colleague lets him buy drinks all around.

I have so far spoken of Lewis's ability to peer into the psyche in its quieter moments. In addition, he has one special knack which is close to melodrama but avoids the taint of the word by its terrifying illusion of reality. This is the depiction of damnation.

The full-length portrait is that of Weston. When we first meet him he seems merely an unusually successful and self-important physicist, who has mastered the principles of interplanetary travel, and is planning to colonize other worlds. He tells the Martians, "To you I may seem a vulgar robber, but I bear on my shoulders the destiny of the human race. Your tribal life with its stone-age weapons . . . has nothing to compare with our civilization. . . . Our right to supersede you is the right of the higher over the lower." [6]

When Weston reappears in *Perelandra* he seems at first little altered. If he is changed at all, it is for the better. He has become a disciple of Emergent Evolution. He no longer wants to exterminate the inhabitants of other worlds. He merely desires to coöperate with the *élan vital* by aiding "the forward movement of Life."

The improvement is illusory. He and Ransom soon drift into an argument about religion (Ransom refusing to regard the *élan vital* as synonymous with the Holy Ghost), and

[6] *Out of the Silent Planet*, p. 146.

suddenly a spasm twists Weston's face; he stares at Ransom and howls,[7] "Ransom, Ransom! For Christ's sake don't let them—" then falls to the earth, tearing up moss by the handful.

As the book progresses one is never quite sure when it is Weston speaking, and when it is his demon. The reader perceives that the scientist is becoming a walking corpse, animated by Satan. After the two men engage in their deadly fist fight and the Un-man—as Lewis now calls him—flees on a large fish, followed on another by Ransom, the poor shell of a human being mumbles: [8] "All the good things are now—a thin little rind of what we call life, put on for show, and then—the *real* universe for ever and ever. To thicken the rind by one centimetre—to live one week, one day, one half-hour longer—that's the only thing that matters."

Ransom, taking this for a description of Hell, points out that no one need go there. Weston will not believe him. "Humanity as a whole knows better. It knows—Homer knew—that *all* the dead have sunk down into the inner darkness: under the rind. All witless, all twittering, gibbering, decaying. Bogeymen. . . . You've noticed that all *pleasant* accounts of the dead are traditional or philosophical? What actual experiment discovers is quite different. Ectoplasm—slimy films coming out of a medium's belly and making great, chaotic, tumbledown faces."

The wretched creature blubbers on. The wind rises, the sea is rough. "Oh, Ransom, Ransom! We shall be killed. Killed and put back under the rind. Ransom, you promised to help me. Don't let them get me again."

[7] *Perelandra,* p. 97.
[8] Pp. 177 ff.

The waves dash them closer to the cliff. Suddenly the evil spirit within the Un-man manipulates the controls. Weston seizes Ransom in a deathlike embrace, and the two go down into the deep water. The final struggle in the cave is not between two men—it is between a man and what had been a man.

The modern temper is not prepared for portrayals of damnation and demonic possession. Perhaps this is why the critics have said so little about Lewis's picture of Weston's gradual loss of humanity and his eventual doom. But the description, chapter by chapter, is so discerningly worked out and so hideously plausible that it is one of the most memorable psychological achievements of any contemporary author.

Several characters in *That Hideous Strength* progress smoothly toward damnation. Wither, the deputy director of the N. I. C. E., carries on his daily duties in a sinister haze—his real self is far away, presumably associating with the macrobes. Even in life he has achieved the power of projecting a ghostlike wraith of himself—his apparition is constantly encountered in the most unlikely places, to the terror of his subordinates.

Frost, less bizarre than Wither, reveals his damnation by an intensification—almost a caricature—of the scientist's mask of cold objectivity. With the passage of time he discovers that he no longer has any motives. He performs actions without asking why. The macrobes issue orders to his subconscious; he obeys.

When disaster overtakes Belbury, he still does not know or ask why he locks himself into a room, piles up inflammable material, pours petrol over it, and strikes a match. The fire licks out to consume his body. Suddenly he knows that escape for the soul, if not for the body, is offered him; that he had been wrong from the beginning [9]—

> He half saw: he wholly hated. The physical torture of the burning was not fiercer than this hatred of that. With one supreme effort he flung himself back into his illusion. In that attitude eternity overtook him as sunrise in old tales overtakes trolls and turns them into unchangeable stone.

I spoke a moment ago of the blank spots in Lewis's understanding of human psychology. Perhaps that is not a fair way of putting it. Final judgment—if such a thing is ever possible—must be reserved for writers conveniently dead. Lewis is very much alive, and if he continues his pace of one book per year, he may fill in some of the apparent gaps by publishing new books before this chapter sees print.

But taking Lewis's books as they stand, it is clear that with one exception—the psychology of damnation—he is most at ease in portraying the minute, almost invisible details of everyday feeling and motivation. He creates no Oedipus, no Lear, to rage with cosmic force across the state.

Being a member of the professional class, he is most successful in dealing with his peers—instructors, scholars, scientists. There is an occasional hint that he has considerable understanding—and liking—for men without an Oxford accent (for example, the delightful tramp in *That Hideous Strength*) but they flit only briefly through his pages.

The modern fondness for romantic love and violent passion is disappointed in Lewis. He tells no tales of irresistible infatuation; no adulteries enliven his books. His one de-

[9] *That Hideous Strength*, pp. 427–428.

tailed picture of married life—Jane and Mark Studdock—is neither idyllic enough to suggest the great lovers of history and fiction, nor unhappy enough to demand the divorce court. He seems never to have made up his mind whether romantic love is a good or bad thing; he gives no indication of seeing in it, as Charles Williams did, a valuable spiritual experience—a sort of earthly foreshadowing of the beatific vision.

In general Lewis does better with the men in his books than with the women, who tend to fall into types: the possessive woman, the sharp-tongued old lady, the whiner. And children are neither seen nor heard.

Few if any of Lewis's characters will pass into folklore; men will not talk of "a Mark Studdock" or "a Dr. Dimble" as they do of "a Don Quixote" or "a Uriah Heap." But I venture to predict one exception. The word "Un-man" will win its way into the dictionary and will seldom be spoken without an inward shiver.

However, Lewis's understanding of human nature cannot be wholly judged from the characters he creates. The best evidence of his piercing insight into minds and emotions is the extraordinary success he has achieved in making the most unlikely people read books about Christianity and like it. His approach is so direct that many authorities on winning friends and influencing people would advise against it. He never sugar-coats, never pretends that a difficult thing is easy. In other words, he treats his readers with such respect that they are astounded and intrigued. In this great age of propaganda and weasel words, his manliness and candor win admiration—and sometimes assent.

19. The Word-Weaver [*]

> *If the people have never shown less taste for good books, it is also true that those capable of writing good books have seldom taken less pains to please the people, or, indeed, so freely insulted them. There are members of the* INTELLIGENTSIA *at present (some of them socialists) who cannot speak of their cultural inferiors except in accents of passionate hatred and contempt. Certainly it is fatal to approach this or any other quarrel with the assumption that all the faults are on one side: and just as certainly, in all quarrels the task of conciliation belongs* JURE DIVINO *to the more reasonable of the two disputants.*
>
> —"High and Low Brows," in *Rehabilitations and Other Essays,* p. 116 n [1]

The twentieth century is remarkable for many things, none of which is more striking than the vast gulf fixed between the highbrows and lowbrows. Picasso for the highbrows, Norman Rockwell for the lowbrows; W. H. Auden for the highbrows, Eddie Guest for the lowbrows. When a rare artist or writer manages to bridge the gulf he is looked upon as an esthetic freak: many highbrows read

[*] This chapter was originally published in the *Living Church,* February 20, 1949.

[1] Oxford University Press, London, New York, Toronto, 1939. By permission of the publishers.

Robert Frost in semi-secrecy because his works are sometimes found on the same shelf with James Whitcomb Riley and Sara Teasdale.

The cleavage is probably a symptom of something deep-seated and unhealthy in the state of modern civilization, but I shall not speculate about that here. The results are sufficiently obvious and are injurious to both the high's and the low's. The lowbrows are spoon-fed a meager ration of ideas in a debased and oversimplified form, and offered esthetic experience on a sentimentally false level. The highbrows are driven together, united by the spirit of coterie, and encouraged to hail the latest eccentricity as a milestone in the progress of the human spirit.

Lewis ought to be the complete highbrow. He is a leading English critic, has a command of Greek grammar which is said to be equal to that of any man in classical Oxford, is well read in philosophy, theology, and pagan mythologies. If he chose to go esoteric, he could produce something a good deal more baffling than Eliot's *Waste Land.*

It is probably true that Lewis's most enthusiastic readers are highbrows or upper-middlebrows. He is a cult figure with many college students, professors, writers, and the like. But his following is by no means all highbrow. I have had a chance to observe that he cuts across all frontiers of high and low, and that one will find his books in homes with almost every conceivable educational and cultural background. He is one of the few modern religious writers who have succeeded in doing this. Reinhold Niebuhr, owing to his complex way of presenting his already complex ideas, is read almost entirely by highbrows; Harry Emerson Fosdick by low- and middlebrows.

Lewis has deliberately worked to bridge the gap, and he

wants to bridge it (this is at least one reason) because he regards the distinction as artificial. One might conjecture another motive. Lewis never calls himself a missionary, but he is one. It would be a strange Christian missionary who regarded only the souls of Ph.D.'s and literary critics as worth saving.

In style, Lewis's books range from the slangy chattiness of the broadcast talks to the more formal style and denser texture of *The Problem of Pain*, but anyone who has read two or three of them could almost unerringly spot him as the author of the others.

The most obvious thing is the ease of the writing: the smooth flow of the sentences, which seem to leap from the author's mind fullgrown (as indeed, they often do; his most casual letters are stylistically like his books).

An easy prose style is commoner among British than American writers. It may be that American essayists and novelists, taken as a whole, have had more of importance to say than their British cousins during the last couple of decades, but it is certainly true that they have said it with more fumbling. American style is always swinging back and forth between the he-man monosyllables of Hemingway, the lyric lushness of Wolfe, and the gobbledegook of government reports and the social sciences. There is no national norm, which the writer can use as his point of departure. That such a norm exists in England is evident if one compares writers as diverse as Aldous Huxley, Evelyn Waugh, and C. S. Lewis. The way they manage the language—with an ease and economy of means that make the reader forget the means and think of the meaning—has an unmistakably British flavor.

Some have tried to explain the superiority of British

prose by the influence of Greek and Latin studied from an early age. This is probably not the whole story, but may well be part of it. To figure out the meaning of a sentence from Cicero is not too great an intellectual feat, but to put it into English that sounds like English is so severe a discipline that original composition in the native tongue henceforth seems a pleasant recreation. Lewis had this work-out, and he also was educated under the essay-a-week tradition at Oxford; as a result he began his writing career with far more actual experience in putting words on paper than the average American student receives in college.

In most of his books Lewis avoids highly technical words as far as possible. If an erudite word must be used, he often supplies a brief definition. The word "monism," for example, is hardly known outside philosophic circles. In *Miracles* he uses it, then immediately translates it by the ingenuous barbarism, *everythingism.*

His vocabulary, with rare exceptions, is that of any reasonably well-educated man; it does not require extensive knowledge in specialized subjects. The sentences are usually short without being choppy. When, for rhetorical effect (as to build up a climax), he uses longer sentences, he handles them with enough skill to keep the conjunctions and relative pronouns from sticking out like dislocated bones.

For a writer on philosophy and theology he is remarkably successful in avoiding vagueness. His favorite device for making the abstract concrete is analogy. The Trinity, to give one instance, is defined by the Council of Chalcedon in language that is a perfect network of abstract words; Lewis takes the concepts of Chalcedon and turns them into the analogy of the cube and six squares.

Often the analogies have an ironic or comic twist. Instead of saying, "we must be spiritually reborn," he says,[2] "We're like eggs at present. And you can't go on indefinitely being just an ordinary, decent egg. We must be hatched or go bad." He compares God's love for man to a man's love for his dog, and points out that we should be complimented when God puts us through a school of spiritual hard knocks. "It will be noted that the man . . . takes all these pains with the dog, only because it is an animal high in the scale —because it is so nearly lovable that it is worth his while to make it fully lovable. He does not house-train the earwig or give baths to centipedes." [3]

One reason for Lewis's success as a writer is undoubtedly his modesty, which I believe to be genuine, and which is revealed frequently throughout his books. He is constantly telling the reader that he is a mere layman and no authority on theology. Sometimes he confesses that he cannot make up his mind between two viewpoints, and offers them both. When he ventures an opinion on some controverted point of orthodox theology, he usually prefaces it with a warning that this is merely what he thinks and he may be wrong.

The tone thus created is calculated to soothe and ingratiate. The reader feels, "At least this fellow isn't trying to shove anything down my throat." Then suddenly, when the reader's guard is relaxed, the other Lewis springs into action—the Dr. Johnson, who is very definite about certain things, and leaps in with both feet.

I recall a non-Christian friend of mine who read *The Case for Christianity* with great enjoyment (admiring its moderate air and sweet reasonableness) until he reached

[2] *Beyond Personality*, p. 42.
[3] *The Problem of Pain*, p. 32.

the point where Lewis, having presented the arguments for Christ's divinity, abruptly said: [4] "Either this man was, and is, the Son of God: or else a madman or something worse. You can shut Him up for a fool, you can spit at Him and kill Him as a demon; or you can fall at His feet and call Him Lord and God."

"I should have known it was all a trap," my friend protested. Trap or whatever one chooses to call it, a large part of Lewis's effectiveness comes from the combination of iron hand and velvet glove. It gives him psychological change of pace and a chance for dramatic emphasis.

I have noticed that Lewis's books often have an unsettling effect on readers who completely disagree with him or are only half in accord. This comes partly from his shrewd understanding of psychology. He knows pretty well what the average reader will be thinking at a given moment, and works to counter it. In the Epilogue to *Miracles* there is a good example of insight into the reader's mind, and Lewis's way of saying the last word and leaving troubling questions behind in the subconscious: [5]

> And yet . . . and yet. . . . It is that *and yet* which I fear more than any positive argument against miracles: that soft, tidal return of your habitual outlook as you close the book and the familiar four walls about you and the familiar noises from the street re-assert themselves.

Going on in this vein, Lewis succeeds in suggesting that the arguments against miracles that are inevitably arising in the reader's mind are automatic reflexes of habit, not reasoned objections. In *The Screwtape Letters* there are

[4] P. 45.
[5] P. 199.

many examples of such psychological astuteness; he makes the adversaries of Christianity seem obscurantist and foggily emotional.

When he lets his imagination roam at will—as in the novels—Lewis's descriptions of strange scenes are as concrete as his exposition of theology. There is no swirling vagueness about the landscapes of Malacandra, and the floating islands of Perelandra are as gaily precise as the illustrations from an illuminated manuscript. For a writer who passionately defends the Romanticists, he is remarkably clear and classical in his feeling for scenery.

The novels bring out Lewis's knack of linking events or things that are far apart in time or space. He is always tying the parts of the universe together. The most arresting—and poetically effective—instance occurs in *Perelandra,* when the Un-man, at the beginning of the death struggle with Ransom, throws back his head and cries out the words he has remembered for nineteen hundred years: *Eloi, Eloi, lama sabachthani.*

The most important reason for Lewis's literary appeal may simply be variety. One reader likes exposition, another prefers fiction, a third goes in for satire or fantasy. Lewis has written a small library, offering half a dozen literary roads to Jerusalem. In this he is wellnigh unique among modern religious writers. I can think of only three rivals: G. K. Chesterton, Charles Williams, and Dorothy Sayers.

To a large extent, as I have said, Lewis bridges the gap between the lowbrows and highbrows. But he also bridges the gaps of temperament that cut across the low-high classification. Like another famous missionary and writer, he is all things to all men.

20. A Bird's-Eye Retrospect *

About one matter there is little controversy. Lewis's position as a very discerning literary scholar and critic has not been seriously questioned. Indeed, his enemies urge him to return to scholarship and stick to it. *The Allegory of Love* and *An Introduction to Paradise Lost* have a permanent place on the graduate reference shelf.

As a poet, Lewis is of no great importance. His nonsense verse is clever; his serious poetry always interesting, but fumbling. He has never reached an individual style; his touch wavers. He has wisely turned to prose.

His status as a novelist is much harder to define. If his three attempts are compared with novels in the main English tradition—say with Dickens, Thackeray, and Hardy—they scarcely seem novels at all. The slice of terrestrial life that he portrays is very slender: the prototypes of most of his characters can be observed in a two-minute walk from Magdalen College to the Eastgate pub. The range of emotions is likewise rigidly limited. The canvas, in so far as it is earthly, is tiny and specialized.

But the catch is there. The main scene is not earth but Deep Heaven. The novels must be judged as mythology, and as a myth-maker Lewis has few rivals in modern times: perhaps the very different Kafka comes most readily to

* This chapter was originally published in *Religion in Life*, Spring issue, 1949.

mind. Lewis's myth is consistent within itself, is linked plausibly to human experience and legends, and glows with translucent beauty. The Middle Ages would have been better able to appreciate it than we are. Perhaps in the future, when the naturalistic tradition of fiction has spent its fury, the three interplanetary novels will stand out as among the handful of books from this period honored with cheap reprints.

His other fanciful books must be considered individually. *The Pilgrim's Regress* is interesting mainly to the scholar bent upon *Quellenforschung.* Heavy, complex, obscure, it is yet the grab-bag from which Lewis snatched the raw materials for his later and much better books.

The Screwtape Letters are *sui generis.* The fantastic element in them is merely framework. The *Letters* are intensely realistic studies of human foibles with reference to the devotional life. The keenness of psychology is such that we may well have before us a permanent religious classic.

The Great Divorce lacks the wit and psychological variety of the *Letters,* and the cosmic richness of the novels. But in its thin, serious way it preaches a sermon that reaches the will and the heart as well as the intellect. It is the sort of book that produces delayed reactions and demands rereadings. It is no *Divine Comedy* in either scope or intensity, but perhaps as close as a modern Christian writer, still inhaling the air of paganism with every breath, can approach to it.

Some of the expository books are composed in what is almost a journalistic spirit, to meet the particular needs of a particular period; others are more specialized and grapple with major stumbling blocks to an acceptance of Christianity. Clearly written, lively, well-mannered, often very entertaining, they are models of theological popularization. But I doubt whether Lewis will be remembered mainly for them. They do not allow him sufficient freedom for his mythopoeic imagination. Of this group, I would give *Miracles* the best chance for longevity.

If we abandon now the attempt to examine Lewis by the literary genres he has essayed, and look at the theology presented in book after book, it is clear that he has been remarkably successful in describing and defending the main Christian tradition. Naturally, he does not satisfy anyone completely. The Roman Catholics detect minor heresies here and there and deplore his unwillingness to acknowledge the unique role of the Papacy. The Fundamentalists are made uneasy by his attitude toward the "literal inspiration of the Bible." Every Christian finds occasional *i*'s he would like dotted and *t*'s crossed. But it is doubtful whether any modern theologian has more effectively concentrated on the main points of agreement. The Christianity he sets forth is the common denominator of the faith held by the great majority of Christians throughout the world.

It is not the faith of the Modernists, and Lewis himself recognizes this. To attempt a theology equally satisfactory to the Modernists and the orthodox is a logical impossibility. It could be little more than ethical culture, and would have to omit the doctrines that orthodox Christians consider the core of their religion. Lewis does not make the attempt. He regards Modernism as a heresy, attacks it as such, and devotes his energies to advancing the main Christian tradition.

This main tradition Lewis presents not only clearly but persuasively. Never leaning upon mere emotion in his arguments, he gives the potential Christian solid intellectual reasons for accepting the ancient faith—and at the same time fights a running battle with all brands of "naturalists." However, he does not leave the matter a purely intellectual one. A subtle fragrance of the Blue Flower is exhaled from his books. Christianity becomes as alluring as a fairy tale, and its grim demands somehow woo the emotions as well as the mind.

He does not do everything. His blueprints for personal morality are clear and usable, but we have seen that he offers little guidance to the Christian concerned with the large-scale application of religion to society. One can read the entire Lewis *corpus* and still not know whether the U. N. is the will of Christ or of the Antichrist; the *eldila* of Deep Heaven converse of many things, but not of labor unions and erosion control. For a Christian social philosophy one turns to Maritain, Niebuhr, Berdyaev, George MacLeod, and many others—not to C. S. Lewis.

Lewis is also of little use to the reader who wants a new synthesis of science and religion to supplement or replace that of St. Thomas Aquinas. Lewis is no obscurantist; he is not against the facts and technique of science. He puts no obstacles in the way of the geologist who also wants to be a Christian. But Lewis's background, as he himself recognizes, is philosophic and literary. He would agree that the task of integrating modern science into the Christian framework, so that each is illuminated by the other, must be undertaken by Christian scientists. A start has been made by such scientists as the astronomer, Sir James Jeans, and the biologist, Lecomte du Noüy. For future attempts of this sort Lewis's books should be invaluable, for they provide the scientist with a clear outline of the Christian *datum*.

Lewis is also of little use in meeting the challenge of Gerald Heard, Aldous Huxley, and the other apostles of eclectic mysticism. One gets the impression that Lewis is slightly antagonistic (or perhaps just bewildered) in regard to mysticism. Some day the relationship between the "perennial philosophy" and Christianity will have to be worked out. This, again, is a job for specialists—an equal familiarity with Christian orthodoxy and all the main traditions of mysticism throughout the world is required.[1]

I mention what Lewis has *not* done, not as a reproach to him, but to suggest to his overardent admirers that an exclusive diet of his works is not wholesome. His books contain all the doctrines "necessary to salvation," but not all the ideas necessary for incarnating Christianity into society. Lewis presents Christianity in an almost chemically pure state; there is also an honored place due to writers who are willing to alloy it with baser metals.

To turn now from what he does not do to what he does. The tone of Lewis's books has sometimes been attacked. A number of reviewers have accused him of lack of compassion. The English philosopher, C. E. M. Joad (before his return to the Anglican Church) inquired why Lewis in *The Screwtape Letters* felt himself entitled to rail so confidently against other people's shortcomings:[2] "Is it perhaps symptomatic that one of the failings of which I can find no adequate treatment in the Letters is that of Pharisaism, in the heart of which lurks the belief that we were sent into the world to air our moral prejudices?" *The*

[1] A book which makes a brilliant start toward this is: Alan W. Watts, *Behold the Spirit: A Study in the Necessity of Mystical Religion*. Pantheon, New York, 1947.

[2] *The New Statesman and Nation,* May 16, 1942.

Great Divorce provoked similar outbursts from several critics.

Now it is a sad truth that the greatest Christian writers have not been filled with compassion at all moments. The theologian would doubtless attribute this to Original Sin, which makes it impossible to be completely Christian for twenty-four hours at a stretch. At any rate, Dante, who was able to lead the reader straight up to the Beatific Vision, was not conspicuously charitable toward the damned souls in Hell. One in particular, Filippo Argenti, inspired such loathing in the Florentine that his only desire was to increase the poor creature's misery.[8] Turning to Virgil he said, "Sir, I'd very much like to see him ducked in this muirch before we leave the lake." And Virgil replied: "Before you see the shore you shall be satisfied; your wish is a very reasonable one." Dante then recorded with quiet contentment: "Shortly after this, I saw the muddy people rend him so handsomely that even now I give praise and thanks to God for the sight."

Lewis is not as good a hater as Dante, but his general attitude toward the unsympathetic characters in his books is one of sufficient coldness—"they're getting what they deserve"—to merit a moment's examination.

The charge of Pharasaism can, I think, be dismissed. "I have all the usual vices: the only virtue (if it is a virtue) which I can claim in any marked degree is a patience, amounting almost to a liking, for bores," Lewis wrote in a letter to his publishers. In his Preface to *The Problem of Pain* he assures his readers that he does not live up to the spartan principles he intends to advocate. His whole manner is of a piece with this; one cannot imagine him follow-

[8] Canto 8.

ing in St. Paul's footsteps and urging his admirers to take him as a model of Christian conduct.

But that does not quite dispose of the matter. It remains true that Lewis's evil characters are depicted with a sort of scientific objectivity; he shows little apparent pity as he watches their progress toward Hell. The explanation probably lies in the "either-or" slant of his thinking, plus his belief in free will. Weston is not compelled to become the incarnation of the Devil: by a series of choices he voluntarily opens himself up. Wither and Frost have trained themselves step by step to be the servants of the macrobes. The apostate bishop has turned from the faith because of intellectual laziness and love of popularity. All of them have made themselves what they are. In Hell they should feel at home, for they have created Hell.

The Blessed Spirits of *The Great Divorce* try every appeal to persuade the Ghosts to stay and thicken up, but when they fail (as almost always they do), they go about their celestial business seemingly as cheerful as ever. The narrator is troubled at their seeming heartlessness, but George Macdonald curtly asks whether he wants to give the makers of misery a veto power over all happiness.[4]

That, then, is the dilemma—how can men be saved if they are able to use their free will to reject salvation? And if they insist on damnation, must everyone else spend an eternity weeping for them? From a logical point of view, I do not see how the dilemma can be solved. The slightly disagreeable feeling that one sometimes gets from Lewis's books—the impression that he is too unmoved at the spectacle of damnation—is the price he pays for intellectual honesty. He tries to see the problem *sub specie*

[4] P. 124.

aeternitatis, and we feel a little presumption in the attempt.

To rule out sentimentalism without destroying compassion is very difficult. And yet, it *can* be done. Charles Williams, in *Descent Into Hell* and *All Hallows' Eve,* follows several characters to their damnation, and somehow his tone throughout is one of grave compassion unmixed with the least trace of sloppy sentimentality. But his ability in this respect is almost unique.

I suspect, though I have no direct evidence, that Lewis's belated reconversion to Christianity sharpens his tone a trifle. He must feel himself a brand snatched at the eleventh hour from the burning. Such a state of mind often impedes charity toward sinners still complacent in their self-created illusions. It seems to me that Lewis pictures damnation a bit more convincingly than salvation—in contrast with Macdonald and Williams, who contrive to make salvation more interesting than its opposite.

The other charges commonly leveled against Lewis are patness, glibness, oversimplification. He is accused of making black too black, white too white.

So far as the broadcast talks are concerned the charge is necessarily true. A series of ten-minute addresses cannot deal with all the *if*'s, *and*'s, and *but*'s. They are maps showing only the larger cities and rivers of the Christian landscape.

In his work as a whole I fancy one does detect a certain trace of patness. The books are neat, orderly, rather like the trim lawns and flower beds of Oxford. Whenever I reread the chapter on "Animal Pain" in *The Problem of Pain* I find myself thinking of the tame deer of Magdalen Park. To Lewis, the "salvation" (if one may use the word) of animals is dependent on their having a kind master, which is fine for dogs and cats and hard on potato beetles. Evelyn Underhill, the well-known Anglican mystic, wrote to Lewis in this regard: [5]

> Where, however, I do find it impossible to follow you, is in your chapter on animals. "The tame animal is in the deepest sense the only natural animal . . . the beasts are to be understood only in their relation to man and through man to God." This seems to me frankly an intolerable doctrine and a frightful exaggeration of what is involved in the primacy of man. Is the cow which we have turned into a milk machine or the hen we have turned into an egg machine really nearer to the mind of God than its wild ancestor? . . . When my cat goes off on her own occasions I'm sure she goes with God—but I do not feel so sure of her theological position when she is sitting on the best chair before the drawing-room fire. Perhaps what it all comes to is this, that I feel your concept of God would be improved by just a touch of wildness.

And there I shall leave it. Lewis, whose mind and imagination explore Deep Heaven, takes a bit of Oxford with him wherever he goes; the landscapes of Malacandra are as geometrical as the quads of Magdalen College; the hierarchy of the ancient planet is logically ordered and easily outlined in a fifty-minute lecture.

Lewis, like every other writer, has the virtues of his defects and the defects of his virtues. If his mind were less tidy he would not be able to describe Christianity as lucidly as he does. But the very tidiness of his mind means that certain wild mysteries may not find lodging in his thought.

[5] Charles Williams, ed., *The Letters of Evelyn Underhill,* Longmans, Green and Co., London, New York, Toronto, 1943, pp. 300–302. By permission of the publishers.

21. One Straw in the Wind

A writer, like any other artist, is half mirror and half crystal ball. His stock in trade is an unusual sensitivity, which sometimes enables him to catch incipient changes in popular attitude before they have become evident to less practised eyes.

If one considers the literature of western Europe and America during the past twenty-five years I think this will become clear. In the nineteen-twenties Remarque and Hemingway debunked war; Sinclair Lewis debunked M. D.'s, ministers, and almost everyone else; all the writers who mattered joined forces in debunking Mrs. Grundy and Queen Victoria. To some extent the age of debunking reflected general disillusionment, but the writers were even more disillusioned than their readers. To take the example of war—it was not until the nineteen-thirties that the man in the street became strongly if temporarily convinced that wars are the creations of vile "merchants of death." The novelists of the 1920's had already implied as much. Whether they influenced the common man of the nineteen-thirties or whether they were merely one jump ahead of him is a question for the sociologists. Perhaps it was a little of both.

In the nineteen-thirties the literary climate radically changed. The high seriousness of social consciousness became dominant. Hemingway heard a bell tolling and discovered that "No man is an Iland, intire of it selfe." Steinbeck wrote the *Uncle Tom's Cabin* of the Oakies. Art went into politics and was busy campaigning for a brave new world when World War II came along and disrupted the carefully laid plans.

Many conflicting tendencies are rampant in the nineteen-forties. Ruthless realism and debunking are far from dead; the school of social consciousness still has vigor. But the truly startling development, to one who remembers the earlier eras, is the rise of religion to a position of intellectual respectability. First-class authors are writing about it, and their books are being read by *avant-garde* connoisseurs of literature as well as by the general public.

The American best-seller list has recently included Toynbee's highly Christian *Study of History* as well as his more recent *Civilization on Trial,* Lecomte du Noüy's essay in natural theology, *Human Destiny,* and Joshua Loth Liebman's synthesis of religion and psychology, *Peace of Mind.* The novelists have followed the same trend. Evelyn Waugh turned from the delightful slapstick of *Decline and Fall* to the haunting depth of *Brideshead Revisited*—a thoroughly Roman Catholic but never didactic novel. Somerset Maugham's novel, *The Razor's Edge,* faithfully mirrors the current interest in Oriental mysticism; on a more sophisticated level we have Aldous Huxley's *Time Must Have a Stop.*

One could go on almost endlessly listing novels by competent writers—if not of the stature of Waugh and Huxley—who have chosen religious themes. The poets, too, show the same tendency. T. S. Eliot, the Dante of *The Waste Land,* became an Anglo-Catholic as long ago as 1927, but was forgiven by the critics until the publication of his *Four*

Quartets in 1943 made it evident that his conversion had permeated his poetry as well as his essays. W. H. Auden, who started out to synthesize Marxism and Freudianism in the nineteen-thirties, returned to the Anglican Church and proceeded to write his unmistakably Christian nativity play, *For the Time Being.*

I do not wish to make too absolute a contrast between the present decade and the two preceding ones. But at the least it is certain that the percentage of capable writers dealing with religion has sharply risen, and that the willingness of the educated—even the sophisticated—to read their books has risen proportionately.

Such is the literary and cultural framework in which Lewis's astonishing popularity fits. He is one of the most brilliant of the religious writers who have suddenly emerged almost in the proportions of a school. To explain why religion has all at once become intellectually respectable and even exciting is beyond the scope of this book and perhaps too complex a problem for any commentator to settle with assurance. I tentatively suggest that the main reason is a new kind of disillusionment. The real religion of Europe and America for over a century has been Science and Progress. Science was not greatly esteemed for its own austere sake, but because it created techniques that speeded up Progress. Progress was the steady, unbroken march toward Utopia. Utopia would consist of three square meals a day, a maximum of comforts, and a minimum of onerous labor. Utopia, in fact, was the imaginary heaven created by the yearnings of a materialistic civilization.

Utopia seems less a thing of next year than it did at the turn of the century. World War I dealt Inevitable Progress a heavy blow; World War II a still more brutal one. The rise of totalitarianism suggested that human nature was not as good as had been thought, nor Progress as inevitable. For several decades the lights of enlightenment have been going out faster than they can be lit.

During the interbellum period the hopes of many were fixed on Soviet Russia, which seemed to be creating the earthly paradise by main force. However, Arthur Koestler's *Darkness at Noon* and *The Yogi and the Commissar,* Victor Kravchenko's *I Chose Freedom,* and the independent but similar testimony of a host of other writers who know Russia at firsthand have dampened the early enthusiasm of fellow-travelers. The Berlin-Moscow pact and Russia's post-war policy have also helped.

The significance of Science has in its turn come in for reëvaluation. To the Victorians it was the good genie that would banish drudgery, produce luxuries for everyone, and increase longevity. Since Hiroshima science has become a symbol of terror. In itself it is morally neutral, but in the hands of men it offers the means for ending humanity's problems by ending humanity.

Utopia postponed, Progress no longer inevitable, Science as much foe as friend—all these things have resulted in a profound disillusionment. With disillusionment the ancient questions return. The intellectual and the man in the street both face what men have always faced: the loneliness of clinging precariously to an impersonal planet, uncertainty of what the next year will bring, the certainty of death.

Religion has traditionally claimed that it can provide the answers—that it can explain man's peculiar status in the animal world and give lasting significance to his life. Now that Inevitable Progress is no longer credible, it becomes psychologically possible for disillusioned secularists to examine the claims of religion.

Something else has happened. During the second half of the nineteenth century it required a powerful act of the will for a thoughtful person to accept a religious viewpoint. The whole tenor of Science, at least as popularly understood, was anti-religious. The discoveries of the astronomers, geologists, physicists, and biologists made the universe seem an overgrown machine. This century has seen a gradual but far-reaching revolution in Science, especially physics. The layman does not understand its intricacies, but he gathers that "probabilities" and "statistical averages" are replacing mechanistic "natural laws." The universe, as viewed from the laboratory, is becoming increasingly mysterious. The new Science does not prove the existence of God, but it leaves room for Him.

Whatever the reasons—and I have certainly overlooked some of them—the trend toward a serious reconsideration of the possible truth of religion is obvious, and is most noticeable of all on the upper intellectual levels. If the writers dealing with religious themes are examined more closely, there appear to be two main streams of religious thought that now have vitality in England and America: eclectic mysticism and Christianity.

Eclectic mysticism—often with a Buddhist or Hindu flavor—is advocated as a religious common denominator by Aldous Huxley, Gerald Heard, Christopher Isherwood, and a small group of other highly distinguished writers.

The Christian writers must be sub-classified. Some strands of Christian thought are poorly represented. Modernist Christianity seems to have lost intellectual power in recent years. Its followers tend either to become outright secularists or else move toward a closer approximation to orthodoxy. "Neo-Orthodoxy" (classical Protestantism—especially Calvinism—stripped of its biblical literalism and somewhat reinterpreted) is brilliantly espoused by such theologians as Karl Barth, Emil Brunner, and Reinhold Niebuhr, but seems to have little foothold outside the seminary and the pulpit. The Quaker tradition of Christian mysticism has produced a very rich crop of books dealing directly with religion, but has not resulted in many "oblique books"—novels, poetry, etc.

Classical Christianity seems to be to the fore if recent literature is any gauge. C. S. Lewis, Dorothy Sayers, Charles Williams (three Anglicans) and Evelyn Waugh and Graham Greene (Roman Catholics) write from a viewpoint of essential orthodoxy, and their religion expresses itself as often as not "obliquely."

Using writers as a crystal ball, it seems likely that the faith of the future—if there is a future and it has a faith—will be either eclectic mysticism or Classical Christianity. Possibly the two will merge into a Christian mysticism. During the Middle Ages Christianity was strongly mystical, and the Heards and Huxleys may be rediscovering a vital part of Christianity.

In any event, Classical Christianity—with or without mysticism—is one of the strongest contenders in the desperate race to replace the discredited secularism now visibly going to pieces. Of all the writers advocating Classical Christianity, none combines versatility, literary skill, and psychological insight so richly as C. S. Lewis. He is peculiarly capable of reaching and influencing the people who will influence the masses day after tomorrow. If Christianity revives in England and America it will not be the work of one man—and perhaps not really the work of man at all. But the odds are that it will bear strong traces of the Gospel according to C. S. Lewis.

Bibliography

(A) Books by C. S. Lewis

Spirits in Bondage, William Heinemann Ltd., London, 1919. (Under the pseudonym of Clive Hamilton.)

Dymer, J. M. Dent & Sons, London, 1926. (Under the pseudonym of Clive Hamilton.) [American edition: E. P. Dutton and Co., New York, 1926.]

The Pilgrim's Regress: An Allegorical Apology for Christianity, Reason and Romanticism, J. M. Dent & Sons, London, 1933; Sheed and Ward, London, 1935; Geoffrey Bles Ltd., London, 1943 (with author's Preface, footnotes, and running headlines). [American edition: Sheed and Ward Inc., New York, 1944.]

The Allegory of Love: A Study in the Medieval Tradition, Clarendon Press, Oxford, 1936; reprinted with corrections, Oxford University Press, London, 1938.

Out of the Silent Planet, John Lane, London, 1938. [American edition: Macmillan Co., New York, 1943.]

Rehabilitations and Other Essays, Oxford University Press, London, New York, Toronto, 1939.

With E. M. W. Tillyard, *The Personal Heresy: A Controversy,* Oxford University Press, London, New York, Toronto, 1939.

The Problem of Pain, Geoffrey Bles Ltd., London, 1940. [American edition: Macmillan Co., New York, 1944.]

The Screwtape Letters, Geoffrey Bles Ltd., London, 1942. [American edition: Macmillan Co., New York, 1943.]

A Preface to Paradise Lost: Being the Ballard Matthews Lectures Delivered at University College, North Wales, 1941, Revised and Enlarged, Oxford University Press, London, New York, Toronto, 1942.

Broadcast Talks: Reprinted with Some Alterations from Two Series of Broadcast Talks . . . Given in 1941 and 1942, Geoffrey Bles, Ltd., London, 1942. [American edition: *The Case for Christianity,* Macmillan Co., New York, 1943.]

Christian Behaviour: A Further Series of Broadcast Talks, Geoffrey Bles Ltd., London, 1943. [American edition: Macmillan Co., New York, 1943.]

Perelandra, John Lane, London, 1943. [American edition: Macmillan Co., New York, 1944.]

The Abolition of Man, or, Reflections on Education with Special Reference to the Teaching of English in the Upper Forms of Schools, Riddell Memorial Lecturers, Fifteenth Series, Oxford University Press, London, 1944; Geoffrey Bles, Ltd., London, 1946. [American edition: Macmillan Co., New York, 1947.]

Beyond Personality, Geoffrey Bles Ltd., London, 1944. [American edition: Macmillan Co., New York, 1945.]

That Hideous Strength: A Modern Fairy-Tale for Grown-ups, John Lane, London, 1945. [American edition: Macmillan Co., New York, 1946.]

The Great Divorce: A Dream, Geoffrey Bles Ltd., London, 1946. [American edition: *The Great Divorce,* Macmillan Co., New York, 1946.]

Miracles: A Preliminary Study, Geoffrey Bles Ltd., London, 1947. [American edition: Macmillan Co., New York, 1947.]

Transposition and Other Addresses, Geoffrey Bles, Ltd., London, 1949. [American edition: *The Weight of Glory and Other Addresses,* Macmillan Co., New York, 1949.]

(B) Books Compiled or with Prefaces by C. S. Lewis

A Religious of C. S. M. V. S.Th., translator, *The Incarnation of the Word of God: Being the Treatise of St. Athanasius* De Incarnatione Verbi Dei. With an Introduction by C. S. Lewis. Geoffrey Bles Ltd., London, 1944. [American edition: Macmillan Co., New York, 1946.]

B. G. Sandhurst, *How Heathen is Britain?* Collins, London, 1946. Preface by C. S. Lewis. Revised and Enlarged Edition, 1948.

C. S. Lewis, *George Macdonald: An Anthology,* Geoffrey Bles Ltd., London, 1946. [American edition: Macmillan Co., 1947.] (Preface by C. S. Lewis and 365 brief excerpts from the works of George Macdonald.)

J. B. Phillips, *Letters to Young Churches: A Translation of the New Testament Epistles.* With an Introduction by C. S. Lewis. Geoffrey Bles Ltd., London, 1947. [American edition: Macmillan Co., New York, 1948.]

Dorothy Sayers and others, *Essays Presented to Charles Williams,* Oxford University Press, London, New York, Toronto, 1947. With a Memoir by C. S. Lewis. (Also contains an essay by Lewis, "On Stories.")

Arthurian Torso: Containing the Posthumous Fragment of The Figure of Arthur *by Charles Williams and a Commentary on the Arthurian Poems of Charles Williams by C. S. Lewis,* Oxford University Press, London, New York, Toronto, 1948.

The list of Lewis's works does not include pamphlets or poems and essays published in periodicals. Most of the latter have appeared in *The Spectator, Time and Tide, Punch,* and *Essays and Studies by Members of the English Association.*

It is possible that Lewis has edited other books than the five

I have listed. They are the ones that I have been able to locate.

Material *about* C. S. Lewis is abundant but disappointing. Most of it consists of book reviews and brief human interest articles. Two of the best sustained studies are: Victor M. Hamm, "Mr. Lewis in Perelandra," in *Thought: Fordham University Quarterly,* Vol. XX, No. 77 (June 1945), and Charles A. Brady, "Introduction to Lewis," in *America,* May 27, 1944 (concluded in the June 10, 1944 issue). Lewis's adversaries have largely confined themselves to sniping. One of the few systematic attempts at refutation is provided by J. B. S. Haldane, "God and Mr. C. S. Lewis," *The Rationalist Annual for the Year 1948,* ed. Frederick Watts, Watts & Co., London.

www.ingramcontent.com/pod-product-compliance
Lightning Source LLC
LaVergne TN
LVHW050640100826
845148LV00011B/1919